HERE'S THE DEAL

Examining The Controversial Issues That
Are Being Talked About Today

Larry Tomczak

Reliance Media

FIRST EDITION

ISBN 978-0-9776534-3-0

Library of Congress Control Number: 2008937305

Published by
Reliance Media, Inc.
2395 Apopka Blvd., #200
Apopka, FL 32703
www.RelianceMedia.com

www.HeresTheDeal.cc

Printed in the United States of America

DEDICATION

Dr. Martin Luther King – Christian leader and civil rights activist

- "I have a dream that my four little children will one day live in a nation where they will not be judged by the color of their skin but by the content of their character." (Civil Rights March in Washington D.C., August 28, 1963)

- "I just want to do God's will. And He's allowed me to go up to the mountain. And I've looked over, and I've seen the Promised Land…so I'm happy tonight. I'm not worried about anything. I'm not fearing any man." (Memphis speech on day before his assassination, April 3, 1968)

I have walked through his boyhood home, read his thoughts and observed his life. He has inspired me to pursue the truth and proclaim it peacefully.

Charles Colson – Christian commentator and founder of Prison Fellowship; former White House staff

- "Christians must see that the faith is more than a religion or even a relationship with Jesus. Christianity is a worldview that speaks to every area of life."

- "I am seeking truth – not therapy. Our faith and our experience teach us that the power that created the universe can provide the answers to today's dilemmas."

I have admired his visiting more than 600 prisons in 40 countries along with his passion for communicating truth. When he was awarded the prestigious $1 million dollar "Templeton Prize for Progress in Religion," he gave it to Prison Fellowship as he does all speaking gifts and book royalties.

CONTENTS

Chapter	Description	Page

CHECKPOINT

"What's this? You've got to be kidding!"

Since we've all grown accustomed to passing through security devices and checkpoints at airports, stadiums, libraries and other public venues, we wanted to ask your cooperation as you begin this book.

Some years ago I (Larry) was passing through Reagan National Airport in Washington D.C. on my way to catch a flight. Amongst the blur of faces, I spotted a kiosk of paperbacks. One caught my eye, *The Disciplined Life* by Richard Shelley Taylor.[1]

Walking by briskly, I went about twenty feet then spun around to go back and check out the little green-covered book with the intriguing title. I knew discipline was not my greatest strength, so I sensed it might be a godsend as well as provide some interesting reading on my flight.

Purchasing the item along with a *USA Today*, I dropped it into my leather bag and proceeded to the flight. Whether I'd ever get around to reading it was dubious (remember my problem), but at least I felt better knowing I was finally doing something to remedy my longstanding shortcoming.

As the flight departed, I suddenly had an inclination to do like I did as a kid when I retrieved the "surprise" from my cereal or crackerjack box. Whoosh – in went my hand and out came the book!

Scanning the table of contents, I noticed the chapter headings: "Discipline – the Key to Power". "Discipline – the Mark of Maturity." The first sentence of the book drew me in like a sideshow barker at a county fair: "THE WORLD BELONGS TO THE DISCIPLINED" (I almost pumped my fist in anticipation).

Then I found it! Near the end of the book was what I was looking for: "HOW TO BECOME A DISCIPLINED PERSON."

"Ah ha! That's it!"

Flipping through the pages I quickly riveted my eyes on the object of my pursuit. Then I gulped and smacked my forehead as these words leapt off the page.

---

1   Dimension Books, Bethany Fellowship, Minneapolis, MN

I will drop all formality and speak directly to the reader. Begin by reading the entire book through, including the Introduction, if you have not already done so. Some of you will spot the title of this chapter while scanning the Contents and, recognizing that becoming a disciplined person is the goal, will suppose that to read only this chapter will be sufficient. Such an attempt may be symptomatic of your need of discipline.

The undisciplined person is forever seeking ways to avoid the arduous grind of solid work and to arrive quickly at his goal by short cuts.

Ouch!

How about you?

As we'll describe in the next chapter, all of us today are being affected by a "hurried spirit" and propensity to skim the surface, grab the goodies and "go for the jugular" in our high-speed, Wi-Fi world. Not that you won't get anything out of this book if you take a haphazard, "chippin' and dippin'" approach, but . . .

HERE'S THE DEAL:

Discipline is not doing *what* you want to do, but doing what you *have* to do to achieve success.

May we suggest that in order to get the maximum benefit from this book, you move through this checkpoint, then read it through from start to finish. 'Do not pass go, do not collect $200,' but go directly to the departure gate. Let's begin.

— PART ONE —

1
IS GOOGLE MAKING US STUPID?

**"Criticism may not be agreeable, but it is necessary.
It fulfills the same function as pain in the body.
It calls attention to an unhealthy state of things."
— Winston Churchill**

A regular feature on The Tonight Show is the *'JayWalking'* segment where giant-jaw Jay Leno strolls down L.A. streets asking passer-bys questions that should be common knowledge. If you've seen it you've probably coughed up your Dorito at the antics and answers displayed.

Starbucks in-hand, and maybe a cell phone in the other, our wide-eyed respondents dart back and forth, stammer and stutter, then finally float their answer with all the assurance of a third grader before Sister Angelina,

"Jesus, ah, was, ah, born in . . . . China?"

"The Star Spangled Banner was written by . . . not sure – Bono?"

"Yeah . . . Princess Diana was married to Sir Paul McCartney!"

"Henry Ford invented the…the…light bulb!"

"The Vietnam War ended when, ah, Lincoln signed the Emancipation Proclamation. No, wait . . . when Reagan told them to tear down the Wall. Right?!"

Night after night the willing participants elicit howls of laughter as they display their ignorance and humiliate themselves on national T.V. Just don't tell anybody how many times you thought, "Sure glad I am not the dude standing there looking like an idiot!"

Granted, Jay and his team probably hand-pick the goofiest interviews, but in reality they're not that far off. As we read current surveys and review the testing results of millions of Americans – especially young people, the news is sobering, especially when it comes to knowledge of history, civics and current affairs.

My wife attended George Mason University (remember their Cinderella basketball team?) in Northern Virginia where we lived for a number of years. A professor there named Ilya Somin authored a paper that has relevance here. The title, "When Ignorance Isn't Bliss: How Political Ignorance Threatens Democracy." Listen to what she said:

> "If voters don't know what is going on in politics, they cannot rationally exercise control over government policy . . . . **Most individual voters are abysmally ignorant of even very basic political information.**"

Her depressing conclusion is being echoed today by scores of commentators, educators, social scientists and concerned leaders in every field. When you also consider the fact that in the 2004 presidential election 83 million eligible voters did NOT even cast a vote, maybe it's time to call "time out."

What's true for the general populace is actually worse when we zero in on the 30 and unders.

In his excellent book, "The Dumbest Generation (How the Digital Age Stupefies Young Americans and Jeopardizes Our Future),"[1] author Mark Bauerlein observes:

> "As of 2008, the intellectual future of the United States looks dim . . . the 70's joke about college students after late-60s militancy had waned still holds.

> "'What do you think of student ignorance and apathy?' The interviewer asks the sophomore.

> "`I dun no and I don't care.'

> "It isn't funny anymore. The Dumbest Generation cares little for history books, civic principles, foreign affairs, comparative religions, serious media and art, and it knows less."

Mark goes on to say that the ramifications for the United States are grave. If lessons in schools are watered down, if less books are read, if malls, movie watching and media celebrities are more the focus than even a basic understanding of the issues and information shaping our world and the future – we're sinking into some deep doo-doo!

---

1 Tarcher/Penguin books 2008

A few years ago, the Intercollegiate Studies Institute released their findings on the state of college students regarding civics (pssst – that's the study of the privileges and responsibilities of citizens). The results weren't pretty.

"The Coming Crisis in Citizenship: Higher Education's Failure to Teach America's History & Institutions" revealed...are you ready? ...college freshman averaged an 'F' on basic topics and the seniors...are you seated? ...ditto!

Still think we should fluff off our buddy Jay and his unsuspecting, sidewalk guests? What's happened with young people? Research reveals the following:

■ Twenty-two percent can name all five of the Simpson cartoon characters yet only 1 in 1000 can name all five First Amendment freedoms (speech, religion, press, assembly and redress of grievances).

■ T.V. and Video games now consume 6 to 8 hours daily.

■ YouTube, Face Book and MySpace distract millions for gobs of time A.M. and P.M.

■ Sixty-five percent aren't proficient in reading – even on-line websites!

■ Nine of the top 10 sites are not educational – they're for social networking.

■ Primary news sources consist of sound bites, on-screen scrolls, Jon Stewart's *Daily Show* and *The Colbert Report*.

■ Cell phone usage and text messaging are off the charts.

■ Pop stars and their quirky lifestyles generate more interest than political issues and global events ("Britney Dyed Her Hair Red – All the Juicy Details." "Brad and Angelina Reveal Their 5 Burping Techniques.")

■ Only 20% of young Americans 18 to 34 read a daily newspaper. Besides the Comedy Central "news" shows, they subsist on computer and cable scrolling headlines or sound-bite swatches sandwiched between celebrity breakups or breakdowns.

Should we be surprised if the overwhelming majority of Americans cannot answer Jay's questions, let alone name their senator, governor or a few of the Bill of Rights? And how about this one: Identify Iraq's placement on a world map ("Sorry, that is Mexico, not Iraq").

Cyber-culture has had disturbing effects on today's under 30s. The younger generation has all the advantages of technology: the Internet's 'information super-highway,' blogs, e-mail, ultra-real and interactive video games, a vast array of cable options like the History & Discovery Channels, instant access to libraries, museums and masterpieces worldwide, Internet connectivity, digital wonders and virtual communities. They have all the opportunities to become the most enlightened generation in history.

Yet, the reality: Instead of becoming an informed citizenry the tendency is to milk the innovations to electronically exchange and download texts, tunes, trivialities and today's latest cell phone photos or celebrity scoop.

"Is Google Making Us Stupip?"

This intriguing title was the cover story of the "Atlantic Monthly" magazine in August of 2008. Listen to some of the honest observations offered by the writer, Nicholas Carr. This hits home for both generations (that's why this book is BY and FOR these back-to-back generations).

"I've had an uncomfortable sense that someone, or something, has been tinkering with my brain, remapping the neural circuitry, reprogramming the memory. My mind isn't going – so far as I can tell – but it's changing. I'm not thinking the way I used to. I can feel it most strongly when I'm reading. Immersing myself in a book or a lengthy article used to be easy. My mind would get caught up in the narrative or the turns of the argument, and I'd spend hours strolling through long stretches of prose.

That's really not the case anymore. Now my concentration starts to drift after 2 or 3 pages. I get fidgety, lose the thread, begin looking for something else to do. I feel as if I'm always dragging my wayward brain back to the text. The deep reading that used to come naturally has become a struggle."

Nicholas went on the describe how going on-line, searching and surfing, research that once took days…well now a few Google searches and wham-o – it's done! A new lifestyle of e-mails, scanning headlines and blog posts, podcasts, skimming from link to link…he's different.

Mentioning his troubles with reading to his friends – it's the same.

BOTTOM LINE: The way he and millions are thinking has changed dramatically!

Do you identify? As your mind has attuned to the information highway, complete with e-blasts, text crawls, pop-up ads, sound bites, bulleted articles and easy-to-scan info-snippets, are you aware this has catapulted you out of being more informed to less? We are sacrificing something and being drained of significant insights of information critical to our decision-making and discerning-of-issues for our future. Relying on computer and the fast-paced info-nuggets, has produced two generations that need a helpful handbook that addresses hot-button issues that can't simply be put on the back burner while we wait.

Voila! That's why this book was written.

As a father and daughter, we have teamed up to give you a concise perspective on today's defining issues, along with common sense principles for discovering solutions. And, if you'll pardon the expression, we determined to 'cut the crap.' Other books may address these issues in a scholarly way (and that's good) but who's reading them? Oftentimes it's the pinheads, already convinced, or policy wonks and NOT the vast majority who need help without all the gobbledygook concepts and challenging terminology.

"I know you understand what you think I said, but I'm not sure you realize that what you heard is not what I meant."[2]

Excuse me!?

Let's follow the K.I.S.S. formula – Keep It Simple Sweetie!

May this handbook help us eradicate some of our stupidity and enable us to think clearly about today's three core issues. We personally believe that Americans are more sophisticated than we give them credit for – if they have the information they need. Then maybe if you're in L.A. and turn the corner to encounter Uncle Jay with his camera crew, you'll be ready to at least *sound* intelligent when you make your nationwide debut.

---

2   Robert McCloskey, U.S. State Department spokesman at one of his regular noon briefings during the worst days of the Vietnam War.

2
WHAT THE HECK HAPPENED?

**"People need to be reminded more than
they need to be instructed."
— Samuel Johnson**

It's a hot and humid summer evening, yet the enjoyment of the sights and sounds at the old ballpark eclipse any discomfort you feel. Nestled in your seat, surrounded by friends, you grab a few more gooified nachos and sip your Diet Coke.

Suddenly, the gentle stirring, standing and stretching begins. The melodic organ music kicks in as you remember, "Oh yeah, it's time for our summertime serenade, 'Take Me Out to the Ballgame!'" You jostle your goodies and stand to your feet, ready for the time-honored, seventh-inning stretch.

Wait! Whoever started this summertime tradition repeated nightly, all over America?

HERE'S THE DEAL: Somewhere back in 1910 at a baseball game in the Nation's Capital between the Washington Senators and the Athletics, our 300 pound 27th President of the United States, William Howard Taft, stood up in the middle of the seventh inning. People dressed more formally in those days so understandably he was hot and most uncomfortable in his cramped wooden chair.

Thinking he was about to exit, the rest of the crowd respectfully stood as well. It was a sort of early "wave" experience. It concluded when he returned his rump to the chair.

The change of position obviously proved beneficial as it was repeated in a subsequent game along with the later added, catchy tune. A tradition was born, thanks to a portly president who probably never knew he was the catalyst for this near hundred year old routine.

Today in America's four hundred year journey as a nation, maybe we'd do well to participate in a collective '7th inning stretch' before resuming the game. It would do us well to not merely pause, take a deep breath, then dig back in for more bickering, bashing, attacking and mocking of politicians and pundits over differing views. America is divided on many fronts, although we are united on at least one thing: **more than 80% of us agree our country is headed in the wrong direction.**

Having witnessed the decline of the British Empire, as well as the collapse of nineteen of twenty-one civilizations (not from outside takeover but from within – moral decline), it behooves us to take stock and try to get moving in the right direction. The ancient cry, "If the foundations are destroyed, what can the righteous do?"[3] reminds us who should lead the way.

Like those who partied on the Titanic, many Americans are unaware of the disaster looming ahead. Multitudes seem to be asleep or in some sort of fog. Others are in denial. Some simply shrug off the warning signs and cite our resiliency, heralding the "inevitable" triumph of the human spirit.

In 2008, Russian literary giant, Alexander Solzhenitsyn, passed away. Some of us may recall his commencement address at my son's alma mater, Harvard University, in 1978 where he warned us about many of today's cultural ills. Challenging us to steer clear of the abandonment of our Christian heritage and to recover our adherence to the Supreme Being who "used to restrain our passions and irresponsibility," this brilliant prophet spoke words we need to heed afresh during these turbulent times.

As co-authors representing the two generations predominantly in place at this juncture in America's history, we state unashamedly **we are not pessimists**. We are optimists! Yet we are also realists. We see the storm clouds on the horizon and know our country is badly divided. The Good Book lays it clearly on the line: "A house divided against itself, will not stand."[4]

THE SUMMER OF LOVE

To understand our nation's cultural decline, we need to rewind the tape to a pivotal time – the 60's – to discover how our freefall started. Beginning with the shocking assassination of President Kennedy, a flickering of Camelot- inspired hope was extinguished. Even though

---

3   Book of Psalms, Chapter 11 verse 3
4   Book of Matthew, Chapter 12:25

the Beatles made their inspirational entrance in 1964, prayer and Bible-reading had been banned from our schools and the "God is dead" pronouncement of 1966 fostered an era of skepticism and cynicism bleeding through our land.

It's not like there was one defining event that triggered our current confusion, but when the turbulent twenty-four months of '67 and '68 erupted on the scene, clues emerge. Cultural analysts call this period a "tipping point."

If you're a "Boomer" – you lived through it.

If you're a "Gen-'X'er or Millennial" – you've heard about it.

In '67, I (Larry) graduated from high school and was a drummer in one of those dime-a-dozen "garage bands" that were everywhere, thanks to the Beatles, Stones, Moody Blues and, of course, Jimi Hendrix ("Purple Haze all in my brain . . ."). We called ourselves, "The Lost Souls" and, you know what? We were!

The year 1967 was dubbed, "Summer of Love."   Scores of us naïve youth fell in line behind pied piper Scott McKenzie as we grabbed our knucklehead buddies and love beads and swayed with the wind all the way to San Francisco. Can you hear that song? "Are You Going to San Francisco? You're gonna meet some gentle people there" (keep going?) . . . "All across the nation, there's a new generation . . . people in motion, people in motion." For those who remember, it almost moves you to put some flowers in your hair.

Millions of us idealistic young boomers and our counterpart "hippies" believed we were ushering in the long-awaited "Age of Aquarius" with all our peace symbols, free love and free speech. American Psychologist, Timothy Leary, took LSD and told us "Turn on, tune in and drop out." Seduced by our foolishness we declared, "Never trust anyone over thirty!" "Hope I die before I get old." Groovy, man. Not much longer and we'd be on our way to sloshing in the mud at Woodstock (can you believe it'll be 40 years?!).

Jim Morrison, lead singer of The Doors, was my idol. I even did a college term paper on his life entitled, "The Amplified Poet" (I got an A!). Imagine how many impressionable youth like me were influenced by his philosophy: "I'm interested in anything about revolt, disorder, chaos, especially activities that appear to have no meaning. It seems to me to be the road to freedom!"

Yeah, right. Slowly but surely, those of us who "sowed the wind – reaped the whirlwind."[5] Years of supposed freedom began to take its toll. The good times began to sour and bite us in the rear end! Time magazine called 1968 "a knife blade that severed past from future."

Casting off restraints to protest and launch the Gay, Women's and Black Power Movements, the Sexual Revolution and the Drug Counterculture, we soon morphed into meltdown. The civil rights movement was a positive initiative, but not everyone was going "hoop de do" about that either. As Richard Harris put it in the popular song, "Macarthur's Park:" "Someone left the cake out in the rain. I don't think that I can take it. 'Cause it took so long to bake it. And I'll never have that recipe again. Oh, nooooo...."

In a few short years, pop idols Joplin, Hendrix and Morrison all were dead – overdosing on drugs, sex and unrestrained 'freedom.' Sexually transmitted diseases started breaking out everywhere. AIDS soon followed. Bobby Kennedy and Martin Luther King, Jr. were assassinated. Student riots paralyzed Chicago. The Altamont Rock Festival degenerated into murderous mayhem right before Mick Jagger's bloodshot eyes. An hour from where I attended college, Kent State erupted in campus shootings over the still simmering Vietnam War. Hippie communities and Gay bathhouses started folding like houses of cards as Barry McGuire sang his number one hit, "Eve of Destruction."

Abortion demands intensified as all the "Make love - not war," "Just live together" mantras spawned unwanted babies (conveniently called unwanted "products" of conception). Soon abortion was legalized (resulting in over 50 million deaths -- the eradication of nearly one-third of the entire generation born since '73!). Gulp.

Divorce laws were liberalized (today 80 percent of divorces are "no fault," translating into 42 million divorces since the end of the 60's). Sexual standards evaporated and resulted in rampant pornography, skyrocketing out-of-wedlock births, one in every four teens strapped with a sexually transmitted disease, drugs, school violence, teen suicide, spousal and child abuse, violent crime and prison overpopulation. All of this proliferating since the now infamous "Summer of Love" soured to a stench.

HERE'S THE DEAL: Principles of morality and common sense that served as the underpinnings of our country for almost four centuries, were discarded as "outmoded" and "restrictive." What began with

---

5   Book of Hosea, Chapter 8:7

Robert Hunt consecrating America to God by planting a cross on Virginia Beach in April of 1607 (prior to the Jamestown Settlement), unraveled before our eyes in a relatively short season of time. In their place were substituted dangerous deceptions that gained popular acceptance in our culture. One internationally known author and advocate for the family for over thirty years identified "six lies" that he believes have taken root:

1. Drug use makes great recreational sport.
2. Premarital, extramarital and traditionally abnormal sex are moral and healthy.
3. There should be no sanctity of human life in law.
4. God is dead (at least make it appear that way by systematically "airbrushing" Him from society).
5. Divorce offers an easy "escape" from marriage.
6. Marriage should be redefined to include same-sex unions.[6]

This expert asks, **"Can anyone seriously deny that these ideas have wreaked havoc on our society over the four decades since they gained prominence?"**

We've got to get real – there's too much at stake for ourselves, our families and our future. If you're a young person reading this information for the first time, it's critical you realize what's happened and that you can help reverse the tide. May you experience some sort of epiphany as you read this book that catapults you onto the front lines of today's battle.

THE RACE FOR THE RELIGIOUS MIDDLE

We are presently smack dab in a season of profound change. We're seeing a "changing of the guard" as older, seasoned leaders are recognizing the newly emerging leaders laying hold of the baton. Our challenge is for both generations to "keep their eye on the ball," so to speak, and work together with their complementary strengths for the future of America.

In this time of transition, people of faith must not abandon their sacred responsibility to the three overarching "core issues" highlighted in this book. Our courage and moral convictions must remain strong while also broadening our focus to include other areas of increasing

---

6   Dr. James Dobson, PhD., Focus on the Family

importance – especially in the sphere of social responsibility. Remember the prophetic warning that Alexander Solzhenitsyn gave in his Harvard address predicting serious consequences for America if we lost our courage. This Russian novelist observed that "from ancient times, decline in courage has been considered the beginning of the end."

We must also be careful that as we broaden our worldview to concern for poverty, AIDS and the environment, we don't drift towards easier, more convenient, "unifier" issues and abandon the three "biggies" that represent the "foundation," the "thread" and the "cornerstone" of our life and future. Savvy politicians courting votes are famous for staking out the familiar "sweet spot" in the middle-of-the road where it's safer, and if we're not vigilant, we (especially the younger generation) can leave the defining issues to the parents. After all, it's important to be more "moderate, progressive and avoid extremism," right?

These three "big issues" do not represent extremism. They represent the heart and soul of our country's present dilemma and our future as a people. In the race for the religious middle, we must stand firm that the more controversial issues remain at the forefront and not get thrown into the soup of "pick-and-choose" your cause!

What are "the big three" issues that must remain pre-eminent? What are the critical, monumental issues that remain before us (even though it sure is tempting to avoid them)?

HERE'S THE DEAL: In these turbulent times, we must embrace a mandate that encompasses the following:

1 - *Propagate the truth regarding our heritage and religious freedom.* This is the FOUNDATION upon which our nation and our history was built.

2 - *Protect the sanctity and dignity of human life.* This is the THREAD that connects all issues of justice and the basis on which they all stand – care for the unborn, elderly, poor, disabled, prisoner, AIDS patient, the sexually enslaved or any of life's most vulnerable.

3 - *Preserve the institution of marriage and family life.* This is the CORNERSTONE upon which the future of our nation and the family stands.

We have to maintain a healthy balance in our sacred responsibility to these three defining issues while also awakening to our responsibility in other vital areas including:

- Racism
- Immigration
- Health care

- AIDS
- Poverty
- Sex trafficking

- Islamic terrorism
- Israel & the Middle East
- Environment & energy

May we inspire each other in an intergenerational effort to deal with these issues, as singer Bono declares, with both CHARITY (genuine care and compassion) and CLARITY (understand the issues and discern truth).

This is why we've taken time at the outset to understand the problem of how we've veered off track. Many people today are either ignorant of the 60's period where many of our "wheels fell off" or are in need of a reality check to bring them out of a sentimental yet distorted remembrance of that time.

REMOVING THE ROMANTIC RECOLLECTIONS

Oftentimes on the Public Broadcasting System (PBS), the viewer-supported network runs fund-raising specials featuring music groups from different decades. Have you seen them? They're most entertaining as The Malt-shop memory-makers of the 50's, the 60's superstars, Do Wop quartets, British bands and others fill the bill. Only one problem, the persuasive pitchman who keeps annoying us at intervals to "Support PBS" and "Keep this great music on the air," is way too young to have lived during the era he's highlighting!

Have you ever seen one of these fund-raiser specials with the grainy footage and well-preserved superstars of yesteryear (well some are well-preserved) when you've surfed the channels at night? Can you picture the dude doing the hawking while you wish he'd be quiet and let us get back to enjoying the program? I almost feel I can time the breaks to jog around the block, take a quick shower and fix myself a nice baloney sandwich on rye before he resumes the clips!

Nostalgically referencing the 60's bands (here comes the Beatles, Stones, Moody Blues and Hendrix again!) he'll wax eloquent and pretend to reminisce . . .

"These are all the original hits...not available in stores...all

digitally remastered.... Oh what a time of peaceful vibes and love. I just feel sooooo moved by the music of these gifted performers who provided the music for such a wonderful time of our lives. Pick up that phone right now and order this 60's music you remember so fondly from the era of peace and friendship. Let all the memories from those years of love and peace begin again as you share them with the whole family."

For those of us who actually lived through those times, some of us almost find ourselves talking to your T.V. set and wanting to smack the guy upside the head. "HEY BUDDY, THAT TIME WAS NOT ALL GROOVY, LOVEY, PEACEFUL, FLOWING-HAIR GIRLS IN GRANNY DRESSES TWIRLING IN THE PARK AMIDST SYRUPY-FACED GUYS WITH TAMBORINES AND DOVES FLYING AROUND THEIR HEADS AS THEY SANG 'KUMBYA' AND PLAYED FLUTES! WE REFUSE TO BE TAKEN IN BY THE ILLUSION!"

HERE'S THE DEAL: We've veered terribly off the path – the pathway of truth! The crisis we're presently in is bottom line, **a crisis of truth.**

THE CRISIS OF TRUTH IN AMERICA

Stated simply, here's the downward spiral we're experiencing - the pattern repeated over and over again throughout history:

- **Reject truth** (results in)
- **Loss of discernment** (which leads to)
- **Moral confusion**

This pattern was outlined by one of the greatest intellects in history; a towering figure named Saul of Tarsus, aka Paul the missionary apostle. In his amazingly preserved, masterpiece letter to the early Roman community, he put it like this:

*"The wrath of God (His righteous anger) is being revealed from heaven against all the godlessness and wickedness of men who suppress the truth (**REJECT TRUTH**) . . . although they knew God, they neither glorified Him as God nor gave Him thanks, but their thinking became futile and their foolish hearts were darkened (**LOSS OF DISCERNMENT**) . . . . They exchanged the truth of God for a lie.... Because of this, God gave them*

over to...[what follows is a cascading list of behaviors including 'shameful acts, perversion, greed, deceit, envy, murder, strife, arrogance, dishonoring parents and inventing ways of doing evil' (**MORAL CONFUSION**)]."[7]

Although it's not pleasant, it's really not that complicated. The insightful words of humanist Mark Twain have particular relevance here:

> "Most people are bothered by those passages in Scripture which they cannot understand; but as for me, I always notice that the passages in Scripture which trouble me most are those I do understand."

Paul's prophetic warning went unheeded by most that lived in Rome. Edward Gibbon's 18th century classic book "The Decline and Fall of the Roman Empire" outlined the reasons for this superpower's demise. Today there are ominous parallels to events in that once-shining "superpower" society:

- Moral decay and craze for pleasure with brutal violence increasing, even as sport.
- Undermining of the dignity and sanctity of the home along with mushrooming divorce.
- Decay of religion – faith fading into mere form
- Higher and higher taxes
- Rampant spending for military armaments

Mr. Gibbon cited the last item on Paul's list, "inventing ways of doing evil," by observing that in Rome's final days, "bizarreness masqueraded as creativity." Sound familiar?

World-respected evangelist Billy Graham told us, "The greatest threat to our culture today is moral degradation."

It's a sobering and scary reality that today the pornography industry alone has gained such a stranglehold on mainstream American culture that it rakes in astronomical profit (exceeding the combined revenues of ABC, CBS and NBC by double!) while poisoning the minds of countless millions. There are 4.2 million sites accessed via 68 billion search engine requests *daily*! Ninety percent of the porn shipped to the world is created in the U.S. (and we wonder why many Muslims seek our downfall!)

---

7   Book of Romans, Chapter 1:18-32.

As porn fuels lust along with other mediums in our country, are we surprised at the skyrocketing rapes, out-of-wedlock births, STDs and abortions? The magnitude of lives lost to abortion alone is staggering if you calculate 50 plus million little babies exterminated since the 73 decision to legalize abortion on demand. That's more than the combined populations of Atlanta, Boston, Chicago, Dallas, Denver, Detroit, Houston, Los Angeles, Miami, Minneapolis, New Orleans, New York, Philadelphia, Phoenix,   San Francisco, Seattle, St. Louis and Washington D.C!

As a result of our *rejection of truth*, then *loss of discernment*, then *moral confusion*, we're on a slippery slope. Undoubtedly, in millions of Americans there exists a vague, persistent and unmistakably real feeling in the pit of our stomachs that all is not well in our land. The German term is "ZEITGEIST." Whatever you label it, it's time to diagnose the problem and declare the solutions.

Here are the three maxims of life that we must learn: (1) Life is a series of choices; (2) Choices have consequences; (3) Choices determine destiny.

Why don't you reread these three. Remember they're true for individuals and societies. Another way of saying this is the timeless "law of sowing and reaping."

Two-thousand years ago, a Roman Governor named Pilate asked Jesus Christ, "What is truth?"

His response revealed the simple mission for which Christ said He came into the world: "I came into the world to testify to the truth."[8] Previously He made this bold declaration, "I am the Way the Truth and the Life."[9]

That's quite a statement. He went on to say that knowing the truth from Scripture and applying it in our lives would bring freedom.[10] Harvard University had this passage as its motto on its original seal (yet later diluted it to be more "politically correct.")

Many people today are having "defining moments" and searching for truth due to the emptiness of their lives or as a result of tragedies and personal failures. Oprah Winfrey observes that many baby-boomers are turning to "spirituality" for answers to that gnawing sense within.

---

8   Book of John, Chapter 18:37-38
9   Book of John, Chapter 14:6
10   Book of John, Chapter 8:31 - 32

Where we live in Tennessee – "Music City U.S.A," many high profile celebrities reside like Keith Urban, Nicole Kidman and Sheryl Crow. Sheryl (9 Grammys and 30 million albums sold) has gone through numerous broken relationships with cyclist Lance Armstrong, actor Owen Wilson and musician Eric Clapton, as well as a highly publicized battle with breast cancer. She has now adopted a little boy. Recently she said something that caught my attention. Remember this is a now 46 year old singer who once crooned "All I wanna do is have some fun:"

> *"My pivotal moment made me want nothing less than the **truth** at all times, and to write about the **truth** and to write from a place of truth and to expect **truth** from my government leaders and the people around me."*[11]

We hear in Sheryl's statement a yearning for reality that we believe is felt by many.

If we are going to help people looking for the authentic as well as regain our footing as a nation and get back on track, then **HERE'S THE DEAL:** WE MUST DISCOVER, DECLARE AND DEMONSTRATE THE TRUTH. This is what people are looking for. This then is our mandate. **"I urge you to contend for the truth."**[12]

Our Creator has revealed truth for us in the Hebrew and Christian scriptures that apply to every area of our lives:[13]

- Career planning.
- Financial management.
- Marriage enrichment
- Mate selection
- Business success
- Child training

- Conflict resolution.
- Effective communication.
- Healthy living.
- Spousal relations
- Solutions to addictions
- Purposeful living

Within our reach are also common sense solutions to today's problems. All we need to do is, to borrow the expression, "look in the book."

Edmund Burke, and 18th century English Statesman, once said, "All that's required for the triumph of evil is for good men to say nothing." He also challenged people of his day to come together into "little platoons" to change their culture for the better.

---

11   "The Tennessean" – July 20, 2008
12   Book of Jude 3
13   Book of 2 Tim., Chapter 3:16 - 17

LITTLE PLATOONS

A "platoon" speaks of a nucleus of like-minded individuals coming together for a cause. One such grouping in history was the "inklings" – a group of writers at Oxford University with J.R. Tolkien, C.S. Lewis and Dorothy Sayers. They sharpened each other's thinking and then wrote books to creatively change their world. Have you appreciated their fantasy fiction classics like the "Hobbit," the "Lord of the Rings" trilogy or the "Chronicles of Narnia?" How about the fantastic films made from these books? Their impact continues to this day.

Another "platoon" was Benjamin Franklin's Junto Society (Junto is Spanish for "assemblies") that met on Friday nights not in a food court or coffee shop, but in homes to generate ideas for changing their world. A few of their accomplishments: the first public library; the concept of volunteer police and fire departments; a public hospital; and, they eventually laid the groundwork to establish a university - the University of Pennsylvania!

British parliamentarian, William Wilberforce, who was recently featured in the nationally released film, Amazing Grace, had a "platoon" aligned with his two goals of ending slavery and reforming the morals of his day. Against all odds, this champion and his platoon witnessed slavery abolished throughout the empire – decades after the battle began! Talk about persistence! Additionally, this nucleus birthed sixty-nine voluntary associations for the betterment of their culture like the Royal Society for the Prevention of Cruelty to Animals, prison reform and British and Foreign Bible Societies.

May these examples provoke us to resist complacency, educate ourselves with the truth and then engage with others in the pursuit of transformation in our communities and this nation. Will you be a change-agent for the good?

As you are armed with the truth, stand up and be counted with others who are passionate and unafraid amidst the challenges before us. As former President John F. Kennedy exhorted us right before the 60's upheaval began, "Ask not what your country can do for you. Ask what you can do for your country."

We may have veered off the right path temporarily, but now is the time to be informed and involved as a difference maker, seeing truth prevail in our land.

CAN ONE LIFE MAKE A DIFFERENCE?

Let's close by asking the question, "Do you believe your one life can make a difference?" Be honest. It's easy to feel insignificant and think "I'm only one person. How can I influence others in such a way as to make a meaningful impact through my life?"

Consider these examples:

I (Larry) was a twenty year old, son of an immigrant, college student, former "Lost Souls" drummer, confused, insecure, uncertain about my future, unhappy living at home in a lower income family, where we had no car growing up, never went on a vacation, my Dad was a janitor, my Mom was a disabled "scrub woman," my sister was depressed and boozing it up after being jilted in a relationship, and worst of all – I WAS A POLACK FROM CLEVELAND, OHIO - whose motto was, "The Best Location in the Nation"!

Then one day a fifty year old black man entered my life through a good deed done to help me out of a jam. His practical kindness led to an invitation to a gathering of sincere Christians in a store-front, ghetto church in the Hough district of Cleveland. That one encounter triggered a chain of events that led to my spiritual awakening and, well, here it is thirty-eight years later and the abundant life I enjoy with my wife of thirty-two years and four wonderful, grown children, all stems from ONE LIFE THAT MADE A DIFFERENCE. "Thanks, Mister Porter!"

One more –

THE "NEXT RONALD REAGAN?"

Have you ever heard of Bobby Jindal? He's the other brown-skinned, son of an immigrant, political leader on the political horizon today.

Bobby is the precocious, brilliant, Oxford Rhodes Scholar presently serving as Governor of Louisiana. He's only 37 years old, yet, is one of the fastest rising "stars" living in a state known for Katrina and a long history of problems. Rush Limbaugh, host of the 20 year old, number one radio talk show in America (20 million listeners daily) calls him, "the next Ronald Reagan."

Raised in a Hindu culture with weekly PUJAS (ceremonial rites), Bobby considered himself "anti-Christian." Then one day, one person came across his path and his life was never the same.

Seems that young Bobby attended a high school dance where a pretty girl named Kathy caught his eye. As the evening wore on they slipped away to a rooftop where they discussed their futures and she told him her aspiration was to one day be a Supreme Court Justice. Her passion astonished him.

Why, he inquired, was this her life goal?

She then proceeded to explain her quest for seeing justice prevail in defense of the unborn. "I was amazed by her compassion and innocence. Kathy's sincere convictions showed me an aspect of charity I had never encountered before."

This one providential "divine appointment" with one little lady totally transformed Bobby Jindal's life. It led him to convert to the Christian faith and dedicate his life in service for his fellow man. He governs his state with over a 73% approval rating. He speaks up for the sanctity of life and the integrity of marriage (he unashamedly voted in Congress for a Constitutional amendment defining marriage exclusively as between a man and a woman). He's making a difference because a young, high school girl of compassionate convictions dared to believe her one life could spell a difference in other's lives.

How about you? Are you ready to be an impact player in your generation?

HERE'S THE DEAL: The time is *now*. It's not hyperbole to say there's an urgency in the air and all hands really are needed on deck! We truly are in a defining moment in our history. We must make some tough decisions or we could end up looking back in five-to- ten years and realize how this country went fundamentally off track. Let's make sure that does not happen.

3

PERSPECTIVE: WHAT IS YOUR WORLDVIEW?

"Ten blind people feeling a different part of an elephant will describe him differently because of one thing - perspective."

How would you like to be awakened one morning to discover someone is suing you for over twenty million dollars? It happened to me. Check this out….

I (Larry) wrote my portion of this book in a secluded section of a public library. As I penned this chapter, I had a weird experience the morning I walked through the lobby to the 'little boys room' to begin my day.

Glancing at a cart of "Free for the Taking" books next to the wall, my eyes descended on a mustard-colored paperback, stopping me dead in my tracks. The title exploded like a 4th of July fireworks display lighting up an ebony sky.

"Oh my gosh!" I thought. "I don't believe it." Although it had been twenty-five years, the flood of memories engulfed me – chillingly and swiftly.

Life-altering lawsuit.

$24.5 million dollar claim.

Days of depositions.

Massive legal fees.

Unwanted and unexpected notoriety.

Atop the book was his name – the author who went for the jugular, Thomas A. Harris M.D. Emblazoned under the title were the words, "#1 Bestseller Changing The Lives of Millions!"

The name of the book?

"I'M OK – YOU'RE OK"

The year was 1982 and overnight I found myself caught in the tentacles of agonizing litigation that just wouldn't go away for nearly four years. Other parties got drawn in due to the nature of the offense. *People* magazine did a two page story (yep – there was my "mug" amidst all the celebrity hot shots!) and the national publication, *Charisma*, featured me on their cover.

Oops, sorry, I didn't clue you in on what started this debacle.

Once upon a time a nationally known speaker heard an internationally known speaker utter some words that somehow made their way to me - who mistakenly conveyed them to a crowd in Chico, California, that then were passed along to a radio station that played them over the air where a lady who knew the good doctor in question, heard them and called him to tell him the following innocuous news: "Doctor some young fella' just told an audience that you're dead."

Slam-dunk.

Bomb detonated.

Toilet overflows.

Now a settlement was eventually reached some forty-eight months down agony road. A lesson painfully learned: Always, ALWAYS, *ALWAYS*, check your facts (and make sure you preface comments with the magic word, "Allegedly").

HERE'S THE DEAL – *from my perspective*. When I first heard the "news" that the author had taken his life, I had no idea what was told me was inaccurate. The sources were of national and international stature; their credibility - world-class.

The reality was they were (excuse the pun) dead wrong.

Remember humorist Mark Twain's classic line upon reading his erroneous obituary one morning in the newspaper? "The reports of my untimely death have been greatly exaggerated." If only the late Dr. Harris had thought it so funny.

All of us guilty parties paid our fine and are today the wiser from an episode we'll never forget. I have since asked forgiveness and subsequently had pleasant conver- sations with Dr. Harris' widow, Amy, while in Sacramento, California, and on the phone.

All of this trauma occurred because of a wrong perspective. That's why having a right perspective is so critical in life's journey.

How about you? Are there some areas in your life where your perspective may be skewed or, dare we say, dead wrong? If your approach to life is one of "I'm OK – You're OK," and you're not interested in anyone helping you gain a right perspective where needed, then it's probably best to read no further. But, if you don't want to take the path of mediocrity ('medi' 'ocre' – half way up the mountain) and want to make sure you have a right perspective on the important issues of life, then lay hold of what follows.

Contrary to what many in our culture propagate, here are the three realities of a worldview that will bring you stability, success and security in life.

1. **Truth exists and is knowable.**

2. **Truth upheld brings blessings.**

3. **Truth disregarded brings consequences.**

This worldview is not based upon subjective experiences, popularity polls or the shifting sands of public opinion. Rather it is firmly grounded in objective, absolute truth – "true truth," if you will. Its basis is divinely revealed truth that is recorded in the Hebrew and Christian Bible. It's unchanging…timeless…rock-solid in make-up, unlike so much of what comes our way today.

You have to decide if you will center your life upon the former (mankind's speculation) or the latter (divine revelation). The rest of your life will simply be the outworking of this choice.

In 2008, the long-pursued presidential ambitions of John Edwards came to a screeching halt. It's doubtful he'll ever recover from the revelation that he committed adultery with another woman, repeatedly lied about it, all while his wife was battling inoperable cancer.

Who was the "other" woman and what was her belief system (in other words, what was her worldview upon which she built her life)?

Rielle Hunter, according to a *Newsweek* magazine article (8/25/08) was a divorced, party girl who was steeped in New Age spirituality. She was a "firm believer in the power of truth" (what truth?) and "fiercely devoted to astrology." Rielle believed (based on what?) that she led "many lives," and that souls enter and escape a "field of consciousness." Finally, she and another fella shared a "genius" idea for a "T.V. show about women who help men get out of failing marriages by having affairs with them."

Ms. Hunter certainly has a right to embrace ideas, so-called "truths" and approaches to life like the above. The tragedy remains where it left her, Mr. Edwards, his wife and family, plus the millions who supported this candidate of "2 Americas."

THIS IS NOT THE KIND OF "TRUTH" WE ARE TALKING ABOUT!

Today there are many people who like to say they are "New Age spiritualists" or "PoMos" – postmodernists. The latter hold that there is no such thing as capital 'T' – "Truth." They want to free society from "rigid" categories and "fixed" meanings for a more subjective approach to life – what "I experience as true" is true for me! Another of the presidential candidates in the 2008 election defined "sin" as "being out of alignment with my values." The problem when "my" values differ from "yours:" how do we have any objective standard? Is Hannibal Lecter not a sinner because his values state 'it's fine to kill and eat people?!'

Almost forty years ago, I (Larry) made a quality decision to base all of my life and the decisions of life upon what the Bible says (not what people think it says or twist it to say). Melanie and my three other grown children, along with my wife of thirty-two years, all are in harmony on this one as are her parents who have been married sixty-three years. As a result we've discovered a life of purpose, joy, peace and security.

In his manual for evolution, Charles Darwin's *Origin of the Species* records these words over two hundred times, "Let us assume." Ask yourself, do you want to base you life on *assumptions* or *certainties*? (Someone once told me not to "assume" because it makes an "ass" out of "U" and "me!")

Let me give you a little more background at this point in our journey.

I (Larry) grew up as a Polish Catholic in a household of four nestled next to Lake Erie in Cleveland, Ohio. My wife, Doris, was German Catholic and one of eight children from Steeler heaven - Pittsburgh, Pennsylvania. Today I identify myself as a Christian with a Catholic background, and am part of a great interracial, intergenerational church in Franklin, Tennessee where we reside.

Years ago I shared my life story in a simple autobiography called, *Clap Your Hands*! To my surprise over a quarter million copies sold – one of which made its way into the American embassy as only one of three books allowed during the Iranian Hostage Crisis of 1979. Don't ask me how it got there; one of the former prisoners simply cited it in her book!

Although God had a central place in our family's life, actually we never read the Bible! Neither did Doris' household. Neither did tens of millions of other Catholics, or for that matter millions of others from different denominations across America.

How about you! Have you read the Bible? It is undoubtedly the most important book in history. It's also the first book ever printed and the perennial best seller of all time.

Whether you embrace it as divine revelation or merely as the treasured wisdom of the ages, this manual provides lots of insight on all of life as well as all the issues we'll tackle in this little book.

So you don't think we're trying to impress anyone with erudite thinking or intimidate readers with too serious and scholarly of an approach, let's lighten up the atmosphere and take a break by engaging in a little Bible quiz. Just for fun, see what you know.

FUNNY AND FASCINATING
THINGS IN THE BIBLE

Q. Who was the greatest financier in the Bible?
A. Noah was floating his stock while everyone else was in liquidation.

Q. Who was the greatest female financier in the Bible?
A. Pharaoh's daughter who went down to the bank of the Nile and drew out a little prophet.

Q. Who was the greatest comedian in the Bible?
A. Samson, he brought down the house.

Q. Where is the first baseball game in the Bible?
A. In the big inning, Eve stole first. Adam stole second. Cain struck out. Abel came in last.

Q. How did Adam and Eve feel when expelled from the Garden of Eden?
A. They were definitely put out.

Q. What is one of the first things Adam and Eve did after they were kicked out?

A. They raised a little Cain.
Q. Which servant of Jehovah was the most proficient lawbreaker in the Bible?

A. Moses, he broke all Ten Commandments at once.
Q. Why didn't Noah go fishing?

A. He only had two worms!
Q. Where is the first recorded Biblical case of constipation?

A. In Kings where it says that David sat on the throne for forty years.

Last one:

Q. What is the best way to live and one day get to heaven?
A. Turn right and go straight, the way God says.

How'd you do?

Kidding aside, it's a fact that there is a lot of illiteracy in our country when it comes to the Bible. Barna Research found the following:

- Fifty-eight percent don't know who preached the Sermon on the Mount.

- Forty-eight percent of all adults didn't know the Book of Thomas isn't in the Bible.

- Seventy percent of adults didn't know that the expression, "God helps those who help themselves" is not in the Bible. (Ben Franklin actually originated this phrase.)

There's also a lot of misunderstanding regarding scripture because some folks take a "salad bar" approach, conveniently selecting passages that support positions while neglecting other more challenging ones. ("Skip that stuff about the poor but lay it on heavy about prosperity.")

Some people are dishonest with scriptures (intentionally or unintentionally). "Where in the Bible does it even mention cocaine or pornography?" "I haven't seen gay marriage in the Bible once!" (This actually came from the current Chairman of one of our political parties.)

Others "cherry pick" verses to defend conduct without taking into consideration the context or the whole of what Scripture teaches on a topic ("A text out of context is a pretext."). The fact is the Good Book doesn't categorically say, "Don't judge;" "Don't dance;" "Don't drink;" "Don't go to war;" "Don't let women minister;" "Don't pray in public;" "Don't enjoy sex;" or dozens of other so-called "prohibitions" many erroneously believe. Neither does it tell us in *every* situation to "turn the cheek;" "hand over our cloak;" "give and expect no return;" or scores of other recommendations that need to be clearly explained in their context.

Sometimes people try to discredit the Bible by mocking its content and citing Old Testament passages that seem silly or severe in application ("Gotta stone that 'homo' if we follow your book!"). What they don't understand is this: There are three types of laws prominent in the Old Testament/Hebrew Bible: 1) Ceremonial, 2) Hygienic, and 3) Moral.

The first two (*ceremonial* and *hygienic*) don't apply anymore for those who are part of the New Covenant since the time of Christ, otherwise there'd be no more football (handling a pig skin was a no-no), no more Saturday sports (violating the Sabbath also a no-no), and the over-40 crowd couldn't approach the altar of God with a disability or during that "time of the month." ("You mean I can go get a Wendy's cheeseburger with bacon, have some Red Lobster jumbo shrimp, or enjoy a Honeybaked ham?" Absolutely!). The *moral* laws do still apply, but *not* for or as a means to being "saved" but to show us our need to be saved.

It really is time to gain a better understanding of the Bible, not primarily as a harsh legalistic code of do's and don'ts but rather, as a guidebook of timeless wisdom. It also provides us with a coherent framework for outlining society's problems then prescribes answers to remedy them.

Our challenge is simple: Will we follow a secular or a scriptural worldview? We believe, "For best results, follow instructions in the manufacturer's handbook." Here's a chart to help you see the two paths.

It's really not that complicated but it does require humility.

CONTRASTING SECULARIST AND SCRIPTURAL WORLDVIEWS

- **SCRIPTURAL**: According to Biblical wisdom and principles.

- **SECULAR**: Latin "Saeculum" (time or age); focused on this age alone; rejecting religion and eternity.

- **WORLDVIEW**: How you view all of life; the lens through which you view reality; your personal belief system.

ISSUE	SECULAR VIEW	SCRIPTURAL VIEW
Truth	Subjective and experiential (what feels right); relative; different sources expressed in different lifestyles.	Revealed and knowable; one divine source; objective; single-minded approach to life.
The Bible	An interesting, old, religious book with some worthwhile stories and insights helpful for those who can understand it.	Timeless and authoritative revealed will of God, sufficient for guiding humanity in every area of live.
The Universe and History	Evolution and man-centered (Humanistic tradition)	Creation and God-centered (Judeo-Christian tradition)

Man's Condition	Inherently good, improving, ever-evolving to a higher state.	Original sinful makeup requires a savior to rescue mankind from our plight.
Source of Problems	Ignorance (if man knew better, he'd be better) or environment (man is a victim).	Fallen condition of humanity; human sinfulness (man must take personal responsibility).
God	Whoever or whatever you'd like him/her/it to be. Denial or uncertainty of existence are options.	Loving Creator, merciful Savior, yet also a righteous Judge revealed *generally* (creation and conscience) and *specifically* (written Word - Bible – Incarnate Word-Jesus).
Plight	Ignorant of human potential yet evolving.	Separated from God (spiritually dead).
Sin	Not recognized or redefined as sickness, addiction or weakness.	Willful choices violating God's commands given for our good and society's stability.
Solution	Legislation and education (tougher laws and judges; more jails, police and treatment) or therapy.	Regeneration (a spiritual "rebirth") emphasis on internal transformation while not ignoring necessary external restraints and deterrents.
Provision	Education, medical science, technology, psychotherapy, etc.	The Person and finished work of the Redeemer.
Jesus	A moral teacher who brought wise instruction and was one of many examples for mankind.	Son of God, Sovereign Lord and Savior of mankind.
Response	Better self through human effort and some spiritual activities.	Yield self to the will of God by changing direction (repent) and trusting God (faith).

Guilt	A conditioned response to behaviors deemed 'unacceptable' or 'abnormal' by individuals or institutions.	Conviction and remorse for sinful conduct intended to lead one to confession and change.
Account-ability	Sin is relative, so either non-existent or designed for 'serious' offenders.	All individuals held responsible for their choices in life.
Respons-Ibility	We are codependent victims — others cause our addictions and problems.	While circumstances and people affect us, each one is ultimately responsible for his own choices.
Orientation	Look out for 'number one' while demanding 'rights' and expecting others to meet needs (entitlement).	Passion to please God while learning to live humbly as an obedient servant to enjoy His blessings.
Change	Live by feelings, make excuses, blame-shift, plead ignorance, rationalize and justify wrong behavior.	Live by Biblical directives to obey God who enables us to put off harmful habit patterns and put on new responses reflecting His character.
Afterlife	Denied, ignored, avoided or relegated to old age. Some may accommodate reincarnation, annihilation or possibility of some realm for all except reprobates and history's worst villains.	At death, body decomposes awaiting a future resurrection (soul reunited with body) while our soul enters either into the presence of God (heaven) or eternal separation (hell) based on one's response to the Gospel and a life authenticating it.
Judgment	Non-existent	Disobedience must be punished while obedience is rewarded by a just and loving God.

Goal of Life	Self-actualization; acquisition of wealth; possibly some charitable efforts to better society and appease one's conscience.	Glorify God and fulfill destiny through a life of service that is pleasing to Him before entering eternity.

QUESTION: WHAT PATH ARE YOU PURSUING?

Let's close by considering two statements from individuals who each choose a different worldview. Think of their lives and what legacy they left from their decision.

"All there is is nature and humanity."
— Karl Marx,
Founder of Communism

"When people stop believing in God, they don't believe in nothing -- they believe in anything."
— G.K. Chesterton,
Prolific auther and
world-renowned literary critic

— PART TWO —

4
FAITH AND POLITICS I
- THE FOUNDATION –

**"Secularists are wrong when they ask
believers to leave their religion at the door
before entering the public square."**
— Barack Obama

RELIGION-FREE ZONE?

"In the beginning God. . . ."[14] These four words launch the first of sixty-six books in the Bible. What better way to begin than right here, especially since we live in a country where 96% of Americans say they believe in God.

When astronaut, Buzz Aldrin, stood on the surface of the moon decades ago, he gasped at the galaxy and let loose these familiar words into the expanse of the universe, "The heavens declare the glory of God; the skies proclaim the work of His hands."[15] He was acknowledging God's existence and His role as Creator.

Today, in America, there exists a small yet vocal and well-financed minority of individuals whose primary goal is to remove any reference to God from the public square and to reshape our country into a religion-free zone. Known as "secularists" (focus on *this* world alone; reject *all* forms of religion), or "secular progressives," along with those who now call themselves the "New Atheists" (rejecting any existence of God), they are on a mission to remove our true Judeo-Christian heritage as a nation, deceive the unsuspecting, and advance their agenda any way possible.

Articulate advocates of the "New Atheism" are Oxford evolutionary scholar Richard Dawkins – author of the New York Times bestseller, "The God Delusion," and freelance thinkers Christopher Hitchens and Sam Harris. Their "beef" comes from the post 9/11 sense that religious fanaticism is a luxury the world can't afford any longer. Dawkins states that religious instruction is a form of child abuse and when asked about

---
14   Book of Genesis, Chapter 1:1
15   Book of Psalms, Chapter 19:1

the origin of life suggests that maybe aliens from outer space arrived to get the ball rolling. Imagine E.T. and his boney-long finger may have sparked life on our planet as we know it!

Richard Dawkins stated in Time magazine his views on good and evil: "Good and evil – I don't believe there is hanging out there anywhere something called good and something called evil." You see, when we dismiss the notion of God, we also need to dismiss truth, since everything is relative...subjective. And if there is no truth then there is no basis for morality – something completely contrary to the Bible and our founders who clearly stated our rights and laws were based on "Nature's God."

Comedian George Carlin, who died in 2008 at the age of 71 (he said he was going to live 'til 90), stated his atheistic philosophy like this:

For those of you who look to the Bible for moral lessons and literary qualities, I might suggest a couple of other stories for you. You might want to look at The Three Little Pigs. *That's a good one. ...I've often drawn a great deal of moral comfort from* Humpty Dumpty. *The part I like the best: "All the king's horses and all the king's men couldn't put Humpty Dumpty back together again." That's because there is no Humpty Dumpty and there is no God. None. Not one. No God. Never was.*

When people say there is no God and/or no such thing as absolute/objective truth ('Amazingly 63% of Americans and only 8% of teens acknowledge there is absolute moral truth.'[16]), we are then left with theory and therapy which characterizes much of America today.

No absolute truth? Let me bring a pizza delivery to your door and withhold the scrumptious delight saying you didn't pay when you did ("That's a lie! It's *always* a lie.").

Or witness someone strap on a bomb to kill innocent children ("That's murder! It's *always* murder.").

Or how about observing someone shove your frail grandparents out of a grocery store line to take their place in line ("That's stealing! That's taking their spot! It's *always* wrong.").

But I thought there were no absolutes?

---

16   Barna, cited in Wall Street Journal – July 9, 2004.

Perhaps some folks are simply "absolutely" off the mark (which, by the way, is the actual meaning of "sin" – missing the mark).

Consequences of abandoning God's truth and immutable standards are seen throughout the Bible and history. Remember what we said about a proper worldview? **(1) Truth exists and is knowable. (2) Truth upheld brings blessings. (3) Truth disregarded brings consequences.**

What's happened in America since the 60's should be our wakeup call lest we slide further down the slippery slope.

What's transpired in Quebec, Canada is another illustration of the principle. Remember, "Don't be deceived. God is not mocked. Whatsoever a man sows, so shall he reap."[17]

In the 60's, something called the "Quiet Revolution" swept through Quebec. In a relative short period the people abandoned their Judeo-Christian values and embraced their "new morality." Today these are the facts: Of all the Canadian provinces, Quebec has the lowest marriage and birth rate; highest abortion, divorce and suicide rate; and, the churches are overwhelmingly barren in what once was a strong Catholic center (sound like much of Europe today?). And its sister city, Montreal, has become a notorious "haven for pedophiles," according to Canada's leading news magazine.

One of history's greatest philosophers was the brilliant leader, Blaise Pascal. He once said that "if there is no God, and you bet your life there is, you've lost nothing. But if there is a God, and you bet your life there isn't, you've made the greatest mistake imaginable."

A highly dedicated champion of the secularists is a multi-gazillionaire named George Soros. He's leader of "MoveOn.org" and releases his resources for candidates and causes promoting his vision of a "new America" similar to that of Europe's Amsterdam. Make no mistake about it, he's powerful and passionate in this pursuit, and he's not alone. There are scores of politicians, celebrities, journalists, authors and entertainers who all play on the same team.

"Hold it, dude, what's so bad about changing America so it's more like the tranquil land of the windmills and wooden-shoe Dutch? They're nice people."

Having been to this country numerous times, let me take you there

---

17   Book of Galatians, Chapter 6:7

while tying in its' significance for this defining moment in our history.

IF WE SNOOZE — WE WILL LOOSE!

A while back I was going to the airport in a van when a twenty-something young man seated behind me related the following account of his pregnant wife's recent death. "While driving home, I simply dozed for a few seconds. Rebounding, I found myself drifting into the next lane and then it was too late. The truck hit her side and I lost the love of my life... and our first child."

Tragedies happen. Some can be prevented, others can't. Wisdom dictates vigilance. In pivotal times, its imperative we don't let our guard down, especially as it relates to the direction of our country.

Do we grasp the significance of the moment? After 9/11 we had our "wake up call" – but how many pushed the snooze alarm and drifted back to sleep? *Everything changed with September 11, and there simply is no going back.*

Not long ago I returned from Amsterdam where I had a distinct "wake up call" and a preview of where America is headed if we don't awaken and reclaim our nation from encroaching secularism. For Americans who cherish our nations' founding values of faith and freedom, I have an urgent message: **"If we snooze – we will lose!"**

Amsterdam, Holland was the launch pad for our nation. Remember where our first settlers came from? The Dutch explorer Hudson first came to New York – officially called "New Netherlands." New York City was "New Amsterdam." Brooklyn... Harlem... the Hudson... derive their names from our ancestors. And what was Holland known for then which continues today?

'Tolerance.'

Tolerance historically meant "respect for other's beliefs." Today it's come to mean "respect for others conduct." In other words: No *absolute* standard of morality. "Every man does what is right in his own eyes."[18]

Where can this approach lead? In Amsterdam, these are now legal:

---

18   Book of Judges, Chapter 17:6

- Abortion on demand
- Euthanasia (mercy killing)
- Forms of infanticide
- Same-sex marriage
- Drugs – (hundreds of coffee shops sell hashish with one's mocha)
- On the street sex shows and open, explicit pornography
- Prostitution – (27,000 "registered" ladies sit in sidewalk display windows)
- Explicit homosexual, lesbian, bi-sexual and transvestite activity
- Public nudity
- Sex-change operations ("gender reassignments") – subsidized by the government
- Age of consent – now 12!
- "Burnout" (drop-out "leave" from work) - rampant and totally financed by tax dollars (most get full salary and can renew in five-year cycles).

Let's amplify just one of the above – say, euthanasia. In the Netherlands, the law on euthanasia is *not limited to adults, nor does an applicant for euthanasia have to be terminally ill.* The Netherlands plans to extend its existing euthanasia law for infants born with malformations. "It's very difficult to avoid this debate," says Jacqueline Herremans, president of the Association for the Right to Die with Dignity. "People are feeling; 'Who is the master of my life? It's not God. It's not the state. It's not the physician. I am the master of my life. And I'm the one to decide if I have to suffer of not.'"

In Europe – take Germany, for example (where they should know better after Nazi eugenics programs killed more than 70,000 physically and mentally challenged before and during World War II), a doctor can supply a willing person with lethal drugs to kill themselves if they so choose. A person doesn't have to be in chronic pain or even be suffering from a terminal illness. He or she may simply not want to be moved to a nursing home. He or she may also be coached by greedy or unscrupulous relatives to "get this thing over with!" Think about it... this could be *you* if America follows suit!

America's future? Secularists say, "Why not?"

Unless we arise humbly and regain our nations' original vision, we can lose the love of our life – America as we once knew her. All our wealth cannot substitute for a nation that is spiritually strong. Remember what our 34th President and war hero Dwight D. Eisenhower once said, "The spirit of man is more important than mere physical strength, and the spiritual fiber of a nation than its wealth."

THE A.C.L.U.

Undergirding secularists and atheists in their goal of "liberating" our nation is the American Civil Liberties Union (ACLU). It is at the forefront with its radical agenda to purge our country of its Judeo-Christian values. Founded in 1920 by Roger Baldwin and Crystal Eastman who had strong communist involvement, the ACLU works relentlessly towards its goals of dismantling and reshaping America into its godless image.

Lest you flick this off with a shrug and a "nothin' to worry about," consider:

The ACLU has more than $250 million in assets and over 2000 lawyers on their team. They march in lockstep using legal intimidation and disinformation to declare that Christianity and Judaism and any religious influence must go. Consider a handful of cases they press:

- Remove even "moments of silence," pregame voluntary prayer and graduation invocations.

- Stop any religious symbolism on any public property.

- Defend distribution of child pornography and remove laws to protect children from registered sex offenders.

- Promote acceptance and education of homosexual behavior in schools while opposing any dissent to Darwinian evolutionary theory or free debate of Intelligent Design.

- Overturn the bedrock institution of male/female marriage to radically redefine marriage and family along same-sex lines.

- Demand jail time for anyone praying in a manner they disapprove of.

- Allow Wiccan witches to open town meetings with their mystical, humanistic "prayer" while blocking attempts of Christians and Jews.

- Force Boy Scouts and Girl Scouts to accept homosexual and lesbians as scout leaders.

Thank God *some* of these cases have been stopped (until the ACLU can retry them under an activist judge). What people need to realize is the nature of this organization that works aggressively to marginalize Biblical values, undermine parental authority, remove protection for our children from predators and pornographers, and undercut the sanctity of human life from conception to natural death.

HERE'S THE DEAL: Opponents of faith and Biblical values are trying to instill fear in people with the smokescreen that people of faith want to establish a "theocracy" – government ruled by the Church. They declare we want to "impose" our views on everybody in our culture so everyone has to blindly follow our religion. Here professor Dawkins says, "...absolutism is far from dead. Indeed, it rules the minds of a great number of people in the world today, most dangerously in the Muslim world and in the incipient American theocracy." [19]

Howard Dean, chairman of the Democratic National Committee, suggested noble people who tried to save the brain-damaged Terri Schiavo from being dehydrated to death were foisting theocracy on everyone. He made this declaration: "Are we going to live in a theocracy where the highest powers tell us what to do?"

When we lived in the Nation's Capital, our daily newspaper was *The Washington Post*. One day we awoke to read their assessment of "religious" people: "largely poor, uneducated and easy to command." (February 1, 1993)

Theocracy?

Poor and uneducated?

Imposing our views?

One of my faith-heroes, the person to whom this book is dedicated (along with M.L.K.) is Chuck Colson, the founder of Prison Fellowship serving inmates around the World. He labels this theocracy accusation for what it is, "*a false and malicious charge, and our critics know it. This is absurd because theocracy is contrary to the most basic Christian teaching about free will and human freedom. Christianity gave the very idea of separation of church and state to the West. Christianity advances not by power or by conquest but by love.*"

---

19   Book: The God Delusion by Richard Dawkins

This doesn't mean God-honoring people are to be passive in the political process, uninvolved in elections, or stop promoting justice and righteous legislation. But change comes primarily through *influencing not imposing.* We proclaim and persuade with timeless truth, in a compassionate, compelling way. That's why this book was written – to help us do just that.

SEPARATION OF CHURCH AND STATE

"But what about our Constitution's mandate to be tolerant and uphold the 'wall of separation between church and state?' Also, people shouldn't think America was basically 'Christian' or 'Bible-based,' right?"

Push the pause button right here and get ready to press the delete button just as fast.

Secularists are working for two goals:

1) Convey the idea that our Founding Fathers intended America free from religion – separated by a 'wall between church and state" – so any religious influence in government must be silenced.

2) Convey the idea that the origins of our country came not from Judeo-Christian adherents but rather a mish-mash of agnostics, deists, atheists and opportunists who came here for material gain.

HERE'S THE DEAL – both of these positions are myths! Don't be deceived.

First, our Constitution was designed to give us freedom of religion – not freedom from religion. That's why the early settlers fled England to come here in the first place! They wanted (1) no State Church like in England, and (2) no interference with religion like in England.

Second, the phrase "wall of separation between church and state" is nowhere to be found in the Constitution! It comes from a letter by Thomas Jefferson ("Jefferson's Letter to the Danbury Baptists" 1/1/1802) assuring readers of a First Amendment "Wall" **preventing government from interfering with religion or denying people's**

right to freely exercise their religion. (Psst...If you aren't sure what the First Amendment States – that's okay: "Congress shall make no law regarding the establishment of religion or the free exercise thereof." Notice the limitation clearly stated is upon Congress – not churches!)

Third, let it be known to those striving to reconstruct an America different than our authentic Judeo-Christian heritage, it's time to reaffirm our origins and honor the faith of our forbearers (we'll do this later this chapter). It was Aristotle who said, "If you would understand anything, observe its beginning and its development."

Finally, tolerance does not translate into believing every view is equal, but rather respecting other's right to hold different views (though they may be terribly wrong - say, if they believe in the tooth fairy or the Lochness monster hoax). All ideas can have *equal hearing* while not having *equal footing.* Then we must have the courage to compassionately communicate truth, based on divine revelation, instead of a namby pamby, politically correct, offend nobody approach. This is why so many people of faith have lost their edge.

Dorothy Sayers, an author and fellow Oxfordite along with C.S. Lewis and J.R. Tolkien, wrote these words that should challenge us.

> *"First, I believe it to be a grave mistake to present Christianity as something charming with no offense to it. Seeing that Christ went about the world giving the most violent offense to all kinds of people, it would seem absurd to expect that the doctrine of his person can be so presented as to offend nobody. We cannot blink at the fact that gentle Jesus, meek and mild, was so stiff in his opinions and so inflammatory in his language that he was thrown out of church, stoned, hunted from place to place, and finally labeled a firebrand and a public danger."*[20]

Oftentimes politicians are asked where they stand on an issue and they'll declare with a mushy smile: "Some of my friends are for it. Some are against it. As for me...I'm for my friends!"

'If we don't stand for something, we'll likely fall for anything.' Having lived in D.C. for twenty-four years, I can tell you firsthand that it is teeming with politicians easily identified by wet fingers. Why? Many live not by principle but polls – they hold those wet fingers up to test which way the wind is blowing!

---

20   Letters to the Dominished Church

IT'S TIME TO EXPOSE THE MYTHS!

We need to dust off the words of President John F. Kennedy who led this nation right before the dramatic downturn of the mid-60's.

"The great enemy of the truth is very often not the lie – deliberate, contrived, or dishonest, but the myth – persistent, persuasive, and unrealistic. Belief in myths allows the comfort of opinion, without the discomfort of thought."

His courage and vision rallied the nation behind decisive statesmanly leadership. It enabled us to put a man on the moon (less than ten years from his bold challenge in May of 1961) and force the Soviet Union to pull its missiles from our Cuban backyard at the height of the Cold War. As James Clarke once said, "A politician thinks of the next election, a statesman of the next generation."

IT'S TIME TO STAND UP FOR THE TRUTH

Think of another great American leader, Dr. Martin Luther King, Jr. who proclaimed the truth fearlessly. He gave his famous "I've Been to the Mountaintop" speech at the historic Mason Temple in Memphis knowing intuitively his stand for racial equality would cost him his life. The night before he was killed he told the people,

"I've seen the promised land. I may not get there.... But I want you to know tonight that we, as a people, will get to the Promised Land."

The next day, he was dead. Dr. King helped secure historic victories in the fight for racial equality. The Civil Rights Act of 1964 banned discrimination in government, employment and housing. The Voting Rights Act of 1965 followed.

Be inspired reading this excerpt from his own autobiography. Imagine, he was only 27 years of age. He had a wife and three small children:

"One night (in January, 1956) I settled into bed late after a strenuous day...as I was about to doze off the telephone rang. An angry voice said, 'Listen nigger, we've taken all we want from you; before next week you'll be sorry'.... I hung up, but I

couldn't sleep. It seemed that all of my fears had come down on me at once. I had reached the saturation point. I got out of bed and began to walk the floor. I had heard these things before, but for some reason that night it got to me. I was frustrated, bewildered...I was ready to give up.... I tried to think of a way to move out of the picture without appearing a coward. I got to the point where I couldn't take it any longer. I was weak.

With my head in my hands I bowed over the kitchen table and prayed aloud, 'Lord, I'm down here trying to do what's right. But Lord, I must confess that I am weak now, I'm faltering. I'm loosing My courage. Now, I am afraid. And I can't let the people see me like this because if they see me weak and losing my courage, they will begin to get weak. The people are looking to me for leadership, and if I stand before them without strength and courage they too will falter. I am at the end of my powers. I have nothing left.'

I could hear the quiet assurance of an inner voice, 'Martin Luther, stand up for righteousness. Stand up for justice. Stand up for truth. And lo, I will be with you even unto the end of the world.' I heard the voice of Jesus saying still to fight on. At that moment, I experienced the presence of the Divine as I have never experienced Him before. Almost at once my fear began to go. My uncertainty disappeared. I was ready to face anything."

Three nights later, his house was bombed (thank God no one was hurt!).[21]

Someone else who stood up for truth was England's Prime Minister, Winston Churchill. During World War II, when Adolph Hitler was steamrolling over Europe (with only England than America next in his quest for world dominion), he arose. I've visited the stark, cinderblock 'war room' in London where I imagined what it was like in England's "darkest hour" as she was bombarded relentlessly by German planes and we faced the extinction of democratic freedoms in all of Europe.

This valiant leader of many of our parent's generation (it wasn't that long ago!) arguably rescued Western Civilization because of his stirring speeches that one can still hear in the midst of the museum. Shhhh... can you hear Sir Winston's booming voice once again?

---

21   Excerpt from "The Autobiography of Martin Luther King, Jr.", pg. 75-76, Warner Books, 1998

"I expect that the Battle of Britain is about to begin. Upon this battle depends the survival of Christian civilization.... If we can stand up to Hitler, all Europe may be free and the life of the world may move forward into broad sunlit uplands. But if we fail, then the whole world, including the United States, including all that we have known and cared for, will sink into the abyss of a new Dark Age.... Let us therefore brace ourselves to our duties, and so bear ourselves that, if the British Empire and its Commonwealth last for a thousand years, men will still say, 'This was their finest hour.'"[22]

It's Time We Learn To Discern!

The four major threats to Western Civilization during this past century are the following:

1) NAZISM

2) COMMUNISM

3) RADICAL ISLAM

4) SECULARISM

The first two appear to be somewhat neutralized, although Communism can rear its ugly head again via China and North Korea. Radical Islam is growing stronger and spreading. Secularism (along with its partner, moral relativism – no standards or moral compass) is encroaching upon every area of life. Our assignment is learning to discern these subtle deceptions that can so easily ensnare unsuspecting masses.

Do you recall the scary "wizard" who spoke so authoritatively to Dorothy and her three friends in the classic "Wizard of Oz?" Cowering in fear, they stood knock-kneed before the dazzling, intimidating, machinery concealing the ominous wizard booming out his threats. They stayed immobilized until they finally discerned something was amiss and peeled back the curtain to discover the short, chubby man deceiving them. As children we breathed a sigh of relief and cheered at the expose'.

HERE'S THE DEAL: Many politicians are masters of manipulation who proclaim promises and persuade the masses in order to get elected. "It's time for real change...a new day is dawning...vote for

---

22   Sir Winston S. Churchill: June 18, 1940--House of Commons on the war situation.

me and we'll find the Promised Land!" If we're not discerning (critical thinkers minus the critical spirit) we can awaken after an election with that "Oh oh, we're not in Kansas anymore" sense in our stomachs. The tornado swept us up in the whirlwind of promises and the rhythm of the rhetoric carried us away. Remember, **if we snooze – we lose!**

Let's make sure it doesn't happen on our watch.

5
FAITH AND POLITICS II

DEMOCRAT, REPUBLICAN, INDEPENDENT, MODERATE, LIBERAL, CONSERVATIVE OR DISCERNING AMERICAN?

"Men make their own history, but they do not make it just as they please; they do not make it under circumstances chosen by themselves, but under circumstances directly found, given and transmitted from the past."
— Karl Marx

In 2008, a commercial ran incessantly on T.V. for Lipitor – a cholesterol-lowering drug, featuring Dr. Robert Jarvik, the inventor of the famous Jarvik-7 artificial heart. Then suddenly the Pfizer Corporation yanked the ad. Do you remember it? Do you know what happened?

Seems that someone discerned that behind the curtain something smelt funny. Investigating, they discovered Doctor Bob was actually a researcher, not a board certified doctor. Scenes of him as a virile, athletic man, rowing downstream weren't him, but a look-alike double. Finally, get this, he hadn't even taken Lipitor 'til weeks *after* he was hired by the pharmaceutical company to the tune of $1.35 million! Seems like Jarvy baby laughed all the way to the bank along with Pfizer 'til the Feds looked behind the curtain.

In an era of increasing deceptiveness, from computer-enhanced cover girls to Oprah-promoted bestsellers that turn out to be shams, we must be vigilant. In the New Testament, Jesus Christ warned us in his prophetic address on the end-times that the number one signpost of the end of the world as we know it would be deception.[23]

Now stop for a second and gear up to grab hold of a three word phrase that you need emblazoned across your consciousness and

---

23   Book of Matthew, Chapter 24

seared into your brain. Visualize a white-hot branding iron, sizzling and smoking, pressing this statement into your mind.

Are you ready?

IDEAS HAVE CONSEQUENCES

Freeze. Look at it again.

Scan it slowly.

Stop – say it aloud.

Again,

Ideas have consequences.

All of us need to understand that *secular ideas* will have consequences for us, our family, our future and this nation. Likewise, *scriptural ideas* will also have consequences for us, our family, our future and this nation.

In 1964, an epic three-hour plus film was released called, "The Rise and Fall of the Roman Empire," starring Sophia Loren, James Mason, Christopher Plummer and Stephen Boyd (Who? Maybe your parents recall!). The opening line that began this classic epic was the following: "The two biggest questions in history are: 1. 'How Rome rose?' and 2. 'How Rome fell?' This is the story. It was not an event but a process. It did not happen overnight."

- Ideas took root and caused Rome's collapse.

- Ideas in Amsterdam and Europe have taken root and we're witnessing the fruit.

- Ideas are taking root in America and we must develop discernment to sort the good from the bad.

HERE'S THE DEAL: Evil has a pattern: First comes ACCOMODATION, then ACCEPTANCE, finally ADOPTION. Survey the scene today in our nation and you'll see how we've witnessed this with drugs, abortion, cohabitation and other moral evils.

As Americans who want to honor God and uphold His ways, we *are also directed* to "speak the truth in love."[24] This means that we are not judging self-righteously or harshly but rather upholding God's

---

24   Book of Ephesians, Chapter 4:15

unchanging standards by which people either judge themselves or ultimately will be judged by God. If someone pushes back by saying, "Who gives you the right to try to impose your values on us?" simply and winsomely reply, "The same right you have to try to impose your values on us! Someone's values have to prevail."

People pushing for greater "tolerance" and an Oprah Winfrey approach of blending the Bible with other religions to create a hodgepodge, feel-good, type of spirituality, must be unmasked. We are not "bigoted," "self-righteous," "narrow-minded" or "intolerant" for rejecting the "salad bar" approach to faith. We also have grown tired of presenting our crumbling culture with an anemic church that is a mile wide and an inch deep!

Grasping the difference between a secular and scriptural worldview, it's wise to ask ourselves, "Should I identify as a Republican, Democrat, Independent, Moderate, Libertarian, Liberal, Conservative, left-wing or right-wing (or how about the whole bird!)?"

HERE'S THE DEAL: 1) You can call yourself whatever you want – just so you know what the heck that identification stands for! And, 2) You always remain a DISCERNING citizen at the core. Get these right and the rest will fall in line.

It's kinda' like buttoning up a shirt. If you miss the first button – every other button gets out of line. Or allow your car to get out of alignment – soon it'll be shake, rattle and roll."

> *"Give to us clear vision that we may know where to stand and what to stand for – because unless we stand for something, we shall fall for anything."*
>
> — *Peter Marshall,*
> *Former Chaplain U.S. Senate*

POLITICS

Political parties are our American way of accomplishing things by coalescing people around particular agendas. United action increases effectiveness.[25] Let an ox pull a cart and he can pull a thousand pounds. Yoke two oxen together and they can pull five-thousand! It's true!

As a boy, I asked my parents what was the difference between a Republican and a Democrat. Being poor (my Dad was a maintenance

---

25   Book of Ecclesiastes, Chapter 4:9-12

man; my mom a cleaning lady; and we never even owned a car), here was their response: "Democrats care about the hard working folks. Republicans are a bunch of big shot, fat cats who are rich." Not too "fair and balanced," right?

Many black Americans gravitate to the Democratic Party based on similar input. Historically, it was Abe Lincoln and the Republican Party that led the way to abolish slavery. Let's remind ourselves that the Rev. Martin Luther King, Jr.'s historic speech was aimed at persuading a resistant *Democratic* Congress to finally act on civil rights legislation. When J.F.K. and President Johnson seized the initiative to advance civil rights in the 60's, the tide basically turned. Today Republicans are working to reverse this trend.

With Hispanics now the largest minority grouping in our nation, can you understand why both parties are trying to capture their vote?

What's critical to keep in mind is this: When you back a candidate, it shouldn't be because he or she is charismatic, "cool" or carries a "label." Learn to ask the difficult and revealing questions like, "What do they stand for? What is their party's platform (issues they support)?"

Example: If you are persuaded to back a candidate who resembles your favorite pop star and enjoys the same kind of burrito you like at Taco Bell, yet embraces a platform supporting cockroach preservation and elimination of all college scholarships, it's time to call "time out."

A discerning citizen should consider five criteria. To help you remember them, we drew up an acrostic 'C.H.E.A.P.' In other words, don't skimp when it comes to these.

Character – Good, bad or suspect?

History – Where'd they come from? What's their background?

Experience – What has it been and for how long?

Accomplishments – What have they achieved - their fruit?

Platform – What issues do they support and oppose?

What's the Difference Between a Liberal and a Conservative?

Conservative: One who wants to conserve/hold on to what's "right."

Liberal: One who wants to liberate/free society from what's "wrong."

Both have merit, yet both can go wrong.

Example: When someone in the past wanted to "conserve" issues like women not voting, blacks not equal, and voting rights restricted, this was not good.

Likewise, when someone wants to "liberate" society from moral standards to reshape America into another Amsterdam, this also is not good.

This is why it is so important we recover what our Founding Fathers intended and what our nation embraced for three and a half centuries prior to the 60's upheaval we discussed. While Jesus is not sitting in heaven waving an American flag and humming "I'm proud to be an American," let's remember that the United States of America has been an example for centuries to the rest of the world. It has modeled a Biblical balance between government authority and individual liberty. It has been a lighthouse of liberty while much of Europe has regrettably sunk slowly into the pit of socialism and moral decline.

Previously Americans enjoyed blessings and balance that was derived from a moral consensus based on a biblical worldview. As people drifted from this orientation, many are now adrift on a sea of moral uncertainty. "Every man does what is right in his own eyes."[26]

Let's call to mind the prophetic warning that President Ronald Reagan made in 1964:

"You and I have a rendezvous with destiny. We will preserve for our children this, the last best hope of man on earth, or we will sentence them to take the last step into a thousand years of darkness."

---

26   Book of Judges, Chapter 17:6

Today we need courageous and compassionate people to winsomely convince folks of our need to recover the core values and convictions upon which our nation was founded while continuing the advances in human rights, concern for the environment, and creating educational and economic opportunity. We need competent leaders of character not those who are basically led about by polls and pundits. Finally, we must discern counterfeit ideas promoted in our culture and declare and demonstrate what is truth.

> *"There are a good many problems before the American people today and before me as President, but I expect to find the solution to those problems just in the proportion that I am faithful in the study of the Word of God."*
> — *Woodrow Wilson, 28th U.S. President*

> *"America was founded by people who believed that God was their rock of safety. I recognize we must be cautious in claiming that God is on our side, but I think it's all right to keep asking if we're on His side."*
> — *Ronald Reagan, 40th U.S. President*

DEMOCRACY OR REPUBLIC?

"What about freedom! Don't we have the right to do **whatever** we want in a democracy?"

Here's the deal: Our Founding Fathers were providentially guided to establish a republic (a body of voting citizens with representatives chosen to serve them) not a pure democracy. Remember the Pledge of Allegiance: "and to the **republic** for which it stands?"

Our founders feared the tyranny of the masses as much as the tyranny of the King! This is why John Adams wrote that unbridled democracy would lead to "everlasting fluctuations, revolts and horrors," finally necessitating police intervention to impose order.

Our republic was basically based upon the Biblical worldview that government is God's instrument for upholding order and what is good, while punishing evil.[27] Our government was established "by the people" to promote and protect the common good. Competent leaders were to be elected as representative "public servants" to serve at the consent of the governed, not beholden to special interest groups (donating

---

27   Book of Romans, Chapter 13:1-7

big bucks to get their way). If a government moves away from this Biblical model and promotes evil rather than good (by allowing culture-destroying laws), it contributes to the culture's decline.

Today, many believe our Government is "out of control." It is urgent that we renew core principles from our founders and regain smaller government, lower taxes and true accountability.

Recognizing the sinfulness of man, our forefathers established checks and balances to power. This is why we have three branches of government: Executive, Legislative and Judicial. "Power corrupts and absolute power corrupts absolutely!"

Our Declaration of Independence was based on Judeo-Christian principles, not guesswork. It mentions God four times:

- "Our Creator"
- "Nature's God"
- "Supreme Judge of the world"
- "Our Divine Protector in whom we rely."

It asserted that all of us are endowed by our *Creator* with certain God-given rights – life, liberty and the pursuit of happiness. *Life* includes the right to life (from conception 'til natural death). *Liberty* does not mean freedom to do whatever one wants, but responsibility to do as one ought (divine and civil laws restrict certain immoral and illegal behavior to balance order and freedom). Example: People can't yell "Fire!" in a crowded theatre, carry guns on planes or run naked through a school. *Pursuit of happiness* includes the privilege to seek (not be handed on entitlement platters) a prosperous, fulfilling life. Happiness did not mean drunkenness, revelry or unrestrained promiscuity.

Our Founding Fathers, honoring a Judeo-Christian belief system, upheld the Hebrew and Christian Bible as their source of wisdom for life, laws and legislation. They unashamedly believed in Divine Providence. They used their collective wisdom to draft documents that clearly reflect a Biblical worldview and have withstood the test of time.

To help us grasp how far we've departed from our roots, imagine the following scenario:

A DISTURBING REALITY

Sitting among your classmates in "Anytown" U.S.A., an attractive looking teacher stands before your public school class to communicate some insights regarding government. Brushing back a wisp of sandy-gray hair from his eyes, he smiles, scans the room, then deliberately speaks.

"I appreciate the opportunity to tell you young men and women some *truths* that we know are *self evident*. Our *God* and our *Creator* whom we know is the *Supreme Judge of the world* and also honored as our *Divine Protector on whom we rely*, is the foundation for three *rights* of *life, liberty* and the *pursuit of happiness*. Remove God and shazaam - you no longer have any basis for any of these rights, and we live by the laws of the jungle. It's not rocket science, is it?!"

KA BOOM! A shockwave ripples through the air as three armed security guards bust open the classroom door and lunge at the instructor, slamming him upside the wall, handcuffing him mercilessly while slapping a piece of duct tape over his mouth.

A collective shriek erupts as students bolt from their seats amidst the shocking intervention.

What is it – a terrorist attack? A child molester finally apprehended? Is he a dangerous criminal – a felon, an escapee that finally was tracked down by local law enforcement and brought to justice? Will this be featured on "America's Most Wanted" or CNN's "Headline News?"

I trust you realize the answer.

HERE'S THE DEAL: The "crime" this public school teacher committed was to reference 'God' in the public classroom where America's secularist elite decided a handful of decades ago that He can no longer even be mentioned. We've erased the very God whom our Founding Father cited as the very source of the very rights we all value so dearly.

Where else do these rights come from? Thin air? Man's imagination? Batman? The Dalai Lama? C'mon – Let's get real.

Either we're honest about their origination or we're left to everyman's interpretation.

Do you see how this recent ouster of God from the public arena amounts to absurdity? *It's born of the intent to establish a religion of secularism as a substitute for the scriptural basis upon which America was founded.*

We have a moral imperative to rectify our current ignorance and waywardness to get back on track. May we pass on to the next generation the same foundation and freedom we baby-boomers received from our parents – those oftentimes called, "The Greatest Generation."

Let's pause and reflect on the immortal words of America's patriot, Samuel Adams (that's not the beer but the man!):

> *"The liberties of our country, the freedom of our civil Constitution, are worth defending at all hazards; and it is our duty to defend them against all attacks. We have received them as a fair inheritance from our worthy ancestors: they purchased them for us with toil and danger and expense of treasure and blood, and transmitted them to us with care and diligence. It will bring an everlasting mark of infamy on the present generation, enlightened as it is, if we should suffer them to be wrested from us by violence without a struggle, or to be cheated out of them by the artifices of false and designing men."*

Today, America has witnessed an erosion of the principles embodied in the Declaration of Independence and enunciated by our Founders. The consequences are confusion and unrest in our land. The challenge is to be discerning of what's happened and reclaim our glorious heritage.

Responding to those who would deny our religious roots and attempt to hijack our heritage, let's end this chapter by letting our history speak for itself.

THE FAITH FACTOR OF
OUR FOUNDING FATHERS

"Blessed is the Nation Whose God is the Lord"[28]

For those trying to establish a new religion of secularism in America, let's refresh our minds with the true heritage of the United States of America. Contrary to what secularists state, our nation was *shaped*

---

28   Book of Psalms, Chapter 33:12

by and, for almost all of its history, *guided by* values and ideals drawn from Biblical Christianity. To teach otherwise is outright dishonesty of the highest degree.

The Founding Fathers, like leaders in the Bible, were not perfect men and some, like most of us, raised doubts about aspects of their faith. Yet they knew in their hearts what Benjamin Franklin stated so well, "Man will ultimately be governed by God, or by tyrants."

Listen as they once-again speak --

"It cannot be emphasized too strongly or too often that this great nation was founded not by religionists, but by Christians, not on other religions but on the gospel of Jesus Christ."
> — *Patrick Henry,*
> *Patriot & Statesman*

"The highest glory of the American Revolution was this: it connected in one indissoluble bond the principles of civil government with the principles of Christianity."
> — *John Q. Adams,*
> *6th President of the*
> *United States*

"Do not let anyone claim the tribute of American patriotism if they attempt to remove religion from politics. If they do that, they cannot be true Americans."
> — *George Washington,*
> *1st President of the*
> *United States*

"There is no country in the world where the Christian religion retains a greater influence over the souls of men than in America.... America is great because America is good. If she ever ceases to be good, she will cease to be great."
> — *Alexis de Tocqueville,*
> *Author of* Democracy in
> America *French observer*
> *of America in 1831*

OUR TRUE HISTORY

- The Mayflower Compact stated the reasons the Pilgrims came to America: "For the glory of God and advancement of the Christian Faith."

- The constitutions of all the original 13 colonies acknowledged God and mandated scriptural education in the public schools. The one textbook used by nearly every public school student was the McGuffey Reader which said, "The Scriptures are especially designed to make us wise unto salvation through faith in Jesus Christ...."

- The 1st Congress began with a 3 hour prayer meeting and Bible study.

- George Washington took his oath of office with his hand on an open Bible and he added his own words, "So help me God" – repeated by every President since.

- Christian chaplains were appointed in the Congress and military, and Bibles were printed at taxpayer expense.

- Our colleges were Christ-centered.

- The U.S. Supreme Court building served as a church every Sunday until the 1850's and during President Thomas Jefferson's two terms, the largest church in America met every Sunday in the U.S. Capital building.

- When the Constitutional Convention was deadlocked in 1787, Ben Franklin called the assembly to prayer, quoting the Bible verse, "Unless the Lord builds the house, the laborers work in vain."[29] Shortly they reconvened and drew up the document that Gladstone called "the most wonderful work ever struck off at a given time by the brain and purpose of man."[30]

---

29   Book of Psalms, Chapter 127:1
30   Mr. Gladstone's Article in The North American Review (Sept. 1878).

INSPIRING QUOTES

"It is the duty of all nations to acknowledge the providence of Almighty God, to obey His will, to be grateful for His benefits, and humbly to implore His protection and favor."
— *George Washington,*
1st President of the United States

"We have no government armed with power capable of contending with human passions unbridled by morality and religion. Our Constitution was made only for a moral and religious people. It is wholly inadequate to the government of any other."
— *John Adams,*
2nd President of the United States

"And can the liberties of a nation be thought secure when we have removed their only firm basis, a conviction in the minds of the people that these liberties are of the gift of God? That they are not to be violated but with His wrath? Indeed I tremble for my country when I reflect that God is just; that His justice cannot sleep forever."
— *Thomas Jefferson,*
3rd President of the United States

"I've lived, sir, a long time, and the longer I live, the more convincing proofs I see of this truth: That God governs in the affairs of men. If a sparrow cannot fall to the ground without His notice, is it probable that an empire can rise without His aid? We've been assured in the sacred writings that unless the Lord builds the house, they labor in vain who build it. I firmly believe this, and I also believe that without His concurring aid, we shall succeed in this political building no better than the builders of Babel."
— *Benjamin Franklin,*
Signer of the Declaration of
Independence and the Constitution

"The Bible is the best of all books, for it is the word of God and teaches us the way to be happy in this world and in the next. Continue therefore to read it and to regulate your life by its precepts."

"Providence has given to our people the choice of their rulers,

and it is the duty, as well as the privilege and interest of our Christian nation, to select and prefer Christians for their rulers."

> — *John Jay,*
> *1st Chief-Justice of the*
> *U.S. Supreme Court*

"Let every student be plainly instructed and earnestly pressed to consider well the main end of his life and studies is to know God and Jesus Christ which is eternal life (John 17:3) and therefore to lay Christ in the bottom as the only foundation of all sound knowledge and learning."

> — *Harvard 1636 Student Guidelines*

"All the scholars are required to live a religious and blameless life according to the rules of God's Word, diligently reading the Holy Scriptures, that fountain of Divine light and truth, and constantly attending all the duties of religion."

> — *Yale 1787 Student Guidelines*

"The Americans combine the notions of Christianity and of liberty so intimately in their minds that it is impossible to make them conceive the one without the other."

"Upon my arrival in the United States, the religious aspect of the country was the first thing that struck my attention; and the longer I stayed there, the more did I perceive the great political consequences resulting from this state of things, to which I was unaccustomed. In France I had almost always seen the spirit of religion and the spirit of freedom pursuing courses diametrically opposed to each other; but in America I found that they were intimately united, and that they reigned in common over the same country."

> — *Alexis de Tocqueville,*
> *French observer of*
> *America in 1831, author of*
> Democracy in America

Celebrating over 400 years ago when explorer Robert Hunt consecrated America to God by planting a cross on Virginia Beach in April of 1607….

Commemorating over 232 years when the Declaration of Independence was ratified in Congress on July 4, 1776….

Let's remind ourselves afresh –

- That the signers of this document risked their personal fortunes as well as their lives to make this declaration.

- That they faced the possibility of a crushing defeat at the hands of the most powerful army and navy in the world at that time.

- **That the average age of a continental army soldier fighting in the American Revolution was 13 years old.**

- That what followed this declaration for these 13 united states were numerous military defeats and hardships of all kinds.

- That in less than 100 years later another even more horrendous was would be fought over the question of equality.

- That not one but two world wars would require the sacrifice of American lives for the preservation of these rights?

- That freedom still requires us to sacrifice.[31]

We're making you a deal, you can't refuse. Prove your gratitude by standing up for true truth and being counted in this critical hour of America's history. Our nation (according to recent polls) is comprised of 76-78% of adults identifying themselves as Christians. Our forefathers saw fit to include "In God we trust" on our money. Let's not sheepishly sit back on our hands and let some in the minority trick us through so-called "restrictions" far beyond our United States Constitution.

---

31   Compiled by Tom Mowbray.

6

ABORTION AND THE SANCTITY OF LIFE I

- THE THREAD -

"Injustice anywhere is a threat to justice everywhere."
— Martin Luther King, Jr.
Letter from Birmingham Jail

CONSTANT CHANGE IS HERE TO STAY

Before revealing the identity of the person who wrote the following words (don't peek or I'll call the Nickelodeon "Slime" folks to get you!), let me give you a few clues. His face is a permanent fixture in the news – it's been that way for thirty years. He twice ran for President of the United States. He marched with Dr. King and was on the balcony when Martin was shot. If you believe, "I am somebody," he may have influenced your life. Maybe you've heard his "Up With Hope. Down With Dope" talks. Finally, he is a strong supporter of abortion…**today**. He changed. He once was a powerfully passionate pro-life politician as a "minister of Jesus Christ."

Guess. Dennis Kucinich? Al Franken? Clint Eastwood?

Nope. It's the Reverend Jesse Jackson. I even had the unique opportunity to speak with him personally years ago! Listen:

"…I was born out of wedlock (and against the advice that my mother received from her doctor) and therefore abortion is a personal issue for me. From my perspective, human life is the highest good, the summum bonum. Human life itself is the highest human good and God is the supreme good because He is the giver of life. That is my philosophy. Everything I do proceeds from that religious and philosophical premise. Life is the highest good and therefore you fight for life, using means consistent with that end. Life is the highest human good not on its own naturalistic merits, but because life is supernatural,

~ 65 ~

a gift from God. Therefore, life is the highest human good because life is sacred."

Jesse also wrote an "Open Letter to Congress" in which he said "as a matter of conscience I must oppose the use of federal funds for a policy of killing infants." When I lived in Washington D.C. for twenty-four years, we always participated in the annual March for Life to call for greater social responsibility regarding unborn children in the womb. In the 1977 March for Life, Jackson asked, "What happens…to the moral fabric of a nation that accepts the aborting of the life of a baby without a pang of conscience?"

Reverend Jackson's compelling statements resonated with me because I too could have been a statistic. I was born with a serious malady that, had it been detected through amniocentesis in the uterus, could have prompted a doctor to suggest abortion – though my Mom would never have consented. I remember hearing once that the phenomenal singer Celine Dion, who was one of over ten children, allegedly could also have been aborted. A catholic priest intercepted the counsel given her Mom regarding abortion and reportedly saved her life. Wow! What a loss that would have been.

What happened with Rev. Jesse? He simply changed his mind when he decided to run for the presidency. The media labeled it "maturing."

In 2008, Jesse had another transformation. After a former Seinfeld comedian used the 'N'-word at a comedy club, the outcry motivated Jesse to call press conferences calling for an end to its usage. There even was a funeral for the 'N'-word at the NAACP Convention. Then Rev. Jackson was caught using the term on a "live" mike during a television break where he whispered Barack Obama should be castrated for telling some blacks to be more responsible and care for their children.

Oops. He later apologized for using "hurtful" words.

CONSTANT CHANGE IS HERE TO STAY

When more knowledge and information is discovered, isn't it good to make changes accordingly? Consider the following.

The 1973 Supreme Court could plead ignorance after their ruling legalizing abortion on demand saying it didn't have access to the scientific breakthroughs of groundbreaking three-dimensional ultrasound images available today. New advanced medical technology provides us with ringside seats for the "American Idol-in-the-Making" Show! Previously, grainy monitors revealed for our squinting eyes little more than an obscure blob. Now cutting-edge scans show eager viewers the miracle of developing dudes and dudettes with perfect arms, legs and thumb-suckin' movements turning graceful somersaults in mama's cozy cocoons.

In light of the technological breakthrough, all of us have a wonderful opportunity to "press the pause button" and reassess our position on abortion in America. To deny the reality of this unmistakable human evidence would be outright dishonest. And to begrudgingly cast doubt, on what is now obvious, is kinda' like Japan's Emperor Hirohito offering his surrender after Hiroshima and Nagasaki: "The war situation has developed not necessarily to Japan's advantage."

Yeah, right.

Adolph Hitler wrote these words in his 1925 biography, Mein Kampf: "The broad mass of a nation will more easily fall victim to a big lie than to a small one." Many in America believe we succumbed to a lie regarding who really is in the womb and what we should do to protect him or her (not "it").

In the 2008 Presidential campaign, in response to the question, "When does human life begin," one candidate said, "At conception" and the other, "That's above my pay grade." Later, when the Speaker of the House was asked the same question on Sunday's "Meet the Press," this ardent Catholic said, "St. Augustine said at three months" (did he?!)... I don't think anybody can tell you when life begins." Immediately Denver's archbishop Chaput, among others, condemned those remarks as inaccurate.

C'mon, **HERE'S THE DEAL**: People didn't really know much about pre-born life in the early centuries. The "ovum" wasn't even discovered 'til the 1800's! Many of these religious leaders were simply giving their "educated guesses."

Robert P. George,[32] in his landmark book, "Embryo," co-authored by Christopher Tollefsen,[33] left out the religious arguments and cited

---

[32]   Professor of Jurisprudence at Princeton; member of the President's Council on Bioethics.
[33]   Professor of Philosophy at the University of South Carolina.

all the current scientific evidence to establish the person-hood of the embryo. Here's their conclusion:

"Human development begins at fertilization when a male gamete or sperm (spermatozoon) unites with a female gamete or oocyte (ovum) to produce a single cell - a zygote. This highly specialized, totipotent cell marked the beginning of each of us as a unique individual."

Millions now believe the time has come to fess up and say, **"HERE'S THE DEAL:** The abortion debate has been permanently and fundamentally recast in ways that are reverberating throughout our land. Seventy-five percent of women seeking an ultrasound of their unborn baby decide today against abortion. Former Democratic U.S. Senator and Georgia's Governor, Zell Miller said he changed his mind on abortion after viewing a sonogram of his great-grandchild.

There's also other information and significant events persuading people to revisit this all-important issue. Heightened public awareness has come from developments likes these:

- Norma McCorvey and Sandra Cano were the central figures at the epicenter of this defining cultural issue of the century. The former is the legal "Roe" of the "Roe vs. Wade" and the latter is the "Doe" of "Doe vs. Bolton" – the two Supreme Court decisions opening the doors for abortion in America. But today they communicate that they were "lied to," "manipulated" and "used" in order to see abortion legalized. They've changed to become ardent supporters of justice for the preborn and together dedicated the National Memorial for the Unborn in Chattanooga, Tennessee (built on the site of a former "clinic" where 35,000 abortions had once been performed).

- Before her death, Mother Teresa spoke at the National Prayer Breakfast in Washington D.C., with the then President of the United States and his wife (abortion supporters) at her side. Responding to those who say abortion spares "unwanted" children, the diminutive nun extended her arms and said, "There is no such thing as an 'unwanted' child. Bring any such child to me. I will find them a home!" She later stated, "We cannot fight credibly against other social and moral ills, including poverty and violence while we tolerate mass killings by abortion."

- Black Americans are awakening to what their leaders are calling

"Black Genocide." Martin Luther King, Jr.'s niece, Alveda King, said that Planned Parenthood which provides 20 percent of all abortions in the U.S. and took in $336 million in government funds[34] (Did you know your tax dollars go here?) has "led the way in eliminating African-Americans to the point where one quarter of the black population is now missing because of abortion." Black women account for 6 percent of the population but 56 percent of abortions. Upon hearing this statistic, many blacks at first stare in denial, then sit in stunned silence.

- Many feminists have changed since it was discovered that the icon of their movement – the woman whose image appears on the Susan B. Anthony $1 coin – opposed abortion, even writing an essay entitled, "The Revolution" about the "horrible crime of child murder." Anthony wanted to eradicate the practice and said, "No matter what the motive, love of ease, or a desire to save from suffering the unborn innocent, the woman is awfully guilty who commits the deed. It will burden her conscience in life, burden her soul in death."

- The organization "Feminists for Life" now produces a bumper sticker "Peace Begins in the Womb" and feminist leaders such as psychologist, author Sidney Callahan share their change of heart in conferences declaring: "Women will never climb to equality and social empowerment over mounds of dead fetuses."

- Doctors and nurses are speaking out having learned that changes in the Hippocratic Oath have slipped into their medical profession. For 2500 years the Hippocratic tradition shaped the practice of medicine with physicians declaring this solemn promise upon entering their service: "**I will give no deadly drug to any, though it be asked of me, nor will I counsel such, and especially I will not aid a woman to procure abortion.**" Medical schools are being challenged where they've dropped the oath or selectively censored out significant parts.

- The War on Terrorism has caused multitudes to take a fresh look at the legacy of President Ronald Reagan for his foresight and resolve regarding Communism and the Cold War. Likewise, people are re-examining his insights on the sanctity of life from his book "Abortion and the Conscience of a Nation" as well as listening to Reagan's son, Michael, who was adopted and shares his Dad's heart. Here are some excerpts from the "Gipper:"

---

34   Fiscal year 2006-07.

o "Make no mistake, abortion-on-demand is not a right granted by the Constitution. No serious scholar, including one disposed to agree with the Court's result, has argued that the framers of the Constitution intended to create such a right."

o "We cannot diminish the value of one category of human life—the unborn—without diminishing the value of all human life."

o "If you don't know whether a body is alive or dead, you would never bury it. I think this consideration itself should be enough for all of us to insist on protecting the unborn."

o "The abortionist who reassembles the arms and legs of a tiny baby to make sure all its parts have been torn from its mother's body can hardly doubt whether it is a human being."

o "As a nation, we must choose between the sanctity of life ethic and the "quality of life" ethic. I have no trouble identifying the answer our nation has always given to this basic question, and the answer that I hope and pray it will give in the future."

o "As a nation today, we have not rejected the sanctity of human life. The American people have not had an opportunity to express their view on the sanctity of human life in the unborn. I am convinced that Americans do not want to play God with the value of human life. It is not for us to decide who is worthy to live and who is not."

o "We cannot survive as a free nation when some men decide that others are not fit to live and should be abandoned to abortion or infanticide. My Administration is dedicated to the preservation of America as a free land, and **there is no cause more important** for preserving that freedom than affirming the transcendent right to life of all human beings, the right without which no other rights have any meaning."

On the Sunday evening prior to writing this chapter, I sat down with my wife to watch *60 Minutes* and was startled by the timeliness of a statement made by a medical doctor serving 25,000 people in Darfur, West Africa. As you are probably aware, concerned citizens everywhere are awakening to the plight of the 2 million refugees and over 300,000 already slaughtered in the genocide of non-Arabic people by the despotic Sudanese government. Steven Spielberg even withdrew as artistic advisor to the 2008 Olympic Games' opening and closing ceremonies due to China's connection with Sudan. The 60-Minutes footage and description of the carnage we watched was mind-numbing.

"Why does this continue?" asked the CBS correspondent.

The response from the dusty, shaggy-haired physician was brief and to the point. **"People say, 'I didn't know.'"**

The images were shocking but necessary to drive home the urgent need for justice amidst the heinous atrocities. Growing multitudes feel the same about our social responsibility to protect preborn children in the womb.

THE VALUE OF THE VISUAL

Educators universally acknowledge the value of visuals when used properly to call attention to a cause. Grisly pictures of the Nazi Holocaust against the Jews or the dehumanizing brutality of black Americans during the civil rights movement were uncomfortable but essential. Remember the producers of "Schindler's List" donating a copy of the movie to every public and private high school in America?

When it comes to the issue of abortion in America, we must not allow ourselves to say anymore, "We didn't know." If we shrink back from viewing graphic photos of what happens in an actual abortion procedure, we can at least view the awe-inspiring visuals of developing pre-born babies now made possible by these extraordinary advances in medical science. Seeing 3D sonograms of a child in the womb sucking his or her thumb at various stages of development is causing scores of Americans to change their position on abortion. So too is the remarkable photo of the 21 week preborn in-utero who grasped the surgeon's finger during corrective surgery for spina-bifida. Did you see it?

Other developments include –

- Doctors in South Dakota are now required to tell a woman considering an abortion that the procedure "will terminate the life of a whole, separate, unique living human being."

- Laws have now been passed reinforcing the reality that the mother-to-be is carrying a person not merely a "product of conception." Remember the Scott Peterson murder trial where he was found guilty of killing *both* his wife and unborn son, whom the couple planned to name 'Connor?'

- Regularly (if you're alert) you'll see news articles like this one:

"*Crowd Lifts Bus Off Pregnant Woman*

Dozens of strangers converged from all directions to lift a 5-ton bus off the body of a pregnant woman in a superhuman effort that managed to save the life of her child but was too late for her.

"Seven months pregnant, Donnette Sanz was crossing on one the busiest intersections in the Bronx on her lunch break Thursday when she was struck by a van whose brakes failed....

*"About 30 people helped lift the bus, and Sanz, 33, was rushed to a hospital, where doctors delivered her **boy** by Caesarean section....*

*"Mourners and neighborhood residents gathered outside the hospital Friday to pray for Sanz and her **child**."*[35]

In the past, much of the abortion controversy has been characterized by uncharitable conduct and mean-spirited rhetoric. Or the focus has been more theoretical than personal. That's changing as more and more people view sonograms and are increasingly supporting a culture of life. People are changing to admit things simply have gone too far regarding permissive abortion. Let's pause to restate the reality: *the number of abortions in America since the 1973 Roe v. Wade Supreme Court decision legalizing abortion on demand now exceeds 50 million. That's the equivalent of more than the combined populations of Atlanta, Boston, Chicago, Dallas, Denver, Detroit, Houston, Los Angeles, Miami, Minneapolis, New Orleans, New York, Philadelphia, Phoenix, San Francisco, Seattle, St. Louis and Washington D.C!*

---

35   New York, Associated Press, 8/16/08.

For the sake of justice and to promote adoption as the alternative (my wife and I adopted an abandoned Korean child almost 25 years ago and our youngest son, Jason, is adopting a Nicaraguan boy), compassionate people including celebrities like Brad Pitt, Angelina Jolie, Sheryl Crow, Madonna and others have been responding in remarkable ways. Britney Spears' teen sister chose to have her baby and movies like "Juno" and "Knocked Up" featured birthing not terminating themes. We know of a couple, the Murphys in Georgia, who have adopted 23 children – all with special needs – in addition to their four birth children!

This is consistent with Christ's call to "love our neighbor" – the expectant mom as well as the innocent, defenseless unborn child. The dignity of human life is the thread involved in all justice-related issues today because it is this life-connection that compels us to protect the poor, disabled, elderly, dying, the prisoner, the AIDS patient, the sexually enslaved or any of life's needy and most vulnerable. "True religion is to care for widows and orphans."[36]

Thousands of crisis pregnancy centers, homes for unwed mothers, adoption agencies, free ultrasound programs and caring church families have emerged across the nation demonstrating genuine compassion to expectant moms. My friend of over 25 years, Dave Everitt, in Phoenix, Arizona, has led a crisis-pregnancy center for over twenty-five years. When Phil Clark from England heard Dave's message in 1983, he returned to establish over 100 centers in the United Kingdom!

HERE'S THE DEAL: *Our Biblical worldview and common decency compel us to no longer be silent but to demonstrate courage like Rosa Parks did when she wouldn't step to the back of the bus. Or when the workers involved with the "Underground Railroad" saved the lives of thousands of slaves in the 1800's. Or when caring Christians risked their lives to hide and save Jews during Hitler's "Final Solution."*

All of this starts with God and the reality that every person is created in His image and has dignity from womb to tomb. This is what gives all of us value and intrinsic worth. It's the basis referenced by our Founding Fathers in our founding documents where they stated God was "Creator," therefore every person has "certain unalienable rights to life, liberty and the pursuit of happiness."

Remember singing as a child, "Red and yellow, black and white, we are *precious* in His sight, Jesus loves the little children of the world?" Taking a stand for the preciousness of life may not always be "cool"

---

36   Book of James, Chapter 1, verse 27.

or "chic" (it will be costly!), and it does reveal the authentic from the counterfeit – those who truly "love the Lord thy God with all their heart and mind and strength and their neighbor as themselves." This is called the "First and the greatest commandment."[37]

This is not a peripheral issue – it is *front* and *center*. It reveals how we as individuals and a nation view each other as human beings. From a Biblical standpoint I believe you can say unequivocally: IT IS IMPOSSIBLE TO BE A TRUE CHRISTIAN AND NOT BE A SUPPORTER AND DEFENDER OF HUMAN LIFE. This should encompass all areas from conception 'til natural death. This is why Abraham Lincoln said decisively, "If slavery isn't wrong, nothing is wrong!" Abortion is an equal, if not greater, injustice. "The Lord hates hands that shed innocent blood."[38]

Let's get real, if our Federal government has laws protecting, with severe penalties, the life of the bald eagle, spotted owl and gray wolf, yet sanctions partial-birth abortions, isn't something wrong with this picture? It's like pulling up to the stoplight and seeing two bumper stickers on the back of a car: "Save The Wales" and "Keep Abortion Safe and Legal" – ("Safe" for whom? Certainly not the baby). This is absurd.

PEOPLE CAN BE WRONG!

- A few decades ago, actual ads on TV said, "More doctors smoke Camel than any other cigarette" as tobacco products were promoted as healthy and refreshing.

- Thalidomide was promoted as a "wonder drug" to help women experience better pregnancies 'til over 3,500 severely deformed babies were born in the early 60's and it was pulled off the market.

- The Supreme Court ruled in the "Dred Scott Decision" that black people were not "persons" in the eyes of the Constitution and could be bought, sold or even killed as property of the owner.

- Adolph Hitler exterminated 6 million Jews, aged, Gypsies, infirm, mentally challenged, epileptics, amputees and Polish people (my Father was born in Poland!) all based on the

---

37   Book of Matthew, Chapter 22, verse 38.
38   Book of Proverbs, Chapter 6, verse 16.

premise "there is such a thing as a life not worthy to be lived."[39] Language was used to soften the stark impact of what was actually happening. The agency carrying people to death camps was called "The Charitable Transport Company for the Sick," and the organization responsible for the killing of undesirable children was named, "The Committee for Scientific Approach to Severe Illness Due to Heredity."

Do you remember us talking about the need to be discerning? Can you see how some verbal sleight of hand through the use of euphemistic terms like "reproductive rights," "women's health services," "removal of fetal tissue" and "women's right to choose" can distract us from the core reality – our social responsibility to protect human life?

Today, "religious" tactics are even being employed. Groups and slogans exist like, "Spiritual Youth for Reproductive Freedom," "Pro-Faith. Pro-Family. Pro-Choice" and "Pro-Choice Spiritual Left." The ruse: sympathize with the goal of seeing abortions reduced as even "concerned, Bible-believing Christians" yet avoid taking a clear stand on the issue. Some politicians deflect attention to woo voters by saying things like, "Let the states decide," or "Personally, I'm opposed but...." (Remember how war criminals employed this tactic after World War II and 9/11, yet were found guilty?)

A candidate for President in 2008 was asked in a Jamestown, Pennsylvania rally what he'd do if one of his daughters got pregnant outside of marriage. His response, "If they make a mistake, I don't want them punished with a baby."

Punished?!

This candidate believes no restrictions should ever be placed on the "right" of a mother to abort her child. May God change his heart and may we pray that we'll see it happen!

Some abortion providers today do a procedure called "selective reduction." Do you know what this is? After all, it sounds harmless, doesn't it?

Amy Richards explained this procedure in an article in "The New York Times" Magazine after she learned she was pregnant with triplets. Realizing it would mean "shopping only at Cosco and buying big jars of mayonnaise," she asked her obstetrician, "Is it possible to get rid of one of them? Or two of them?"

---

39   Leo Alexander – Office of Chief of Counsel for War Crimes in Nuremberg, 1947.

Her boyfriend balked as he stared at the three preborn babies on the sonogram. "Oh my gosh," he said, "there are three heartbeats. I can't believe we're about to make two disappear."

Amy fluffed off his request to at least consider having the triplets, and aborted the two unborn babies. Without the abortions, she exclaimed, "I'd have to give up my life!" Amy is the brain behind Planned Parenthood's T-shirt campaign encouraging ladies to proudly proclaim, "I Had an Abortion!"

Do you remember what we said earlier about "bizarreness masquerading as creativity?"

Do you remember the progression we cited of *rejecting truth* leading to *loss of discernment* and then *moral chaos*? C'mon, we really do need to stop and say, "Enough is enough!"

- Babies are being aborted up until the day of birth in this country.

- In Wichita, Kansas, you can stand outside the abortion "clinic" of Doctor Tiller and watch the black smoke belch from the smokestack of his furnace and winch at the sickening smell of burning flesh from incinerated bodies of 7th, 8th and 9th month old babies being "disposed."

- **Partial-birth-abortions are supported by politicians (though finally stopped by law) where a live baby comes out and while his head is still in the cervix, a doctor inserts scissors into the back of his head, opens them, sticks a suction tube into the hole and sucks the baby's brains out! I'm sorry, but there simply is no other way to convey this horror than to spell it out.**

What's happened today is basically *misguided freedom* run amuck. It's time to rein things back in, get back on the truth track and defend the weak and needy ones – the "least of Christ's brethren."[40]

Will you step up and be counted?

The Good book tells us clearly, "Have nothing to do with unfruitful works of darkness, but instead expose them. For it is shameful to even speak of the things which are done by them in secret."[41]

---

40   Book of Matthew, Chapter 25, verse 45
41   Book of Ephesians, Chapter 5, verse 11-12.

This is serious stuff. History will judge us most severely if we don't have the backbone to respond. This sanctity of life ethic will impact us all as we age, the population grows, and voices clamor for "solutions" regarding "difficulties" at the other end of the age spectrum. May we not be so naïve as to think we won't personally reap what we sow if we fail this test.

Upholding the sanctity of life ethic honors the "thread" that runs through all of life – from the little preborn child through the disabled, the AIDS victim, the prisoner, the poor, the elderly and the dying. It was this theme that motivated world-change author C.S. Lewis to write his prophetic essay, "The Abolition of Man." In it he referred to the "thread of life" that if disregarded for "the power of man to make himself what he pleases" allows "the power of some men to make other men what *they* please…. Man's final conquest proved to be the abolition of man."

It is time for change. Like MTV's "The Real World" tagline, "It's when people stop being polite and start getting real." Let's stay polite but get real about rectifying what has to rank as the most serious and colossal blunder of this past generation.

Apathy will no longer do. As Helen Keller, the American reformer who herself was blind and deaf since 19 months, once said, "Science may have found a cure for most evils, but it has found no remedy for the worst of them all – the apathy of human beings."

Martin Luther King, Jr. who wholeheartedly supported the sanctity of life, said it best: **"Our lives began to end the day we become silent about things that matter."** May we as Americans shake off any apathy and speak out for justice and the unborn. Let's be at the vanguard of a historic turnaround that history will record.

For those squeamish about mixing religion and politics, know that people of faith weren't jostled out of a nap to finally get involved in the political process when faced with the '73 Roe vs. Wade decision. Sanctity of life has been upheld since the first century when the Didache (early believers handbook) taught, "In accordance with the precept of the teaching, 'you shall not kill,' you shall not put a child to death by abortion or kill it once born."

Let's close with a true, interesting, story. This is especially apropos for those who ask, "What about the 'Save the life of the mother' exception?"

On NBC's Today *Oct.23, pro-abortion host Bryant Gumbel was caught a bit off guard when he interviewed Albert and Angela Valencia and their four-year-old daughter Priscilla. The story was about mother Angela's falling to the floor, unconscious and bleeding internally, when the child phoned 911 for help – a call that saved Angela's life. Mr. Gumbel asked the smiling Priscilla a series of yes/no questions, "Are you always so smart?...Were you pretty scared?...Were you able to tell the man on the other end everything he needed to know?...Did you know your address?...You knew your phone number, you knew everything? Pretty smart little girl, aren't you?"*

He interviewed the father and the 911 operator and everything was going smoothly when he returned to mother Angela. You must be very proud of Priscilla," Mr. Gumbel said. "I am. I am," Angela Valencia replied. "I do want to add, when I was lying in the hospital, I could only remember thinking back because I had Priscilla pretty young, at 15." Counselors told her, "Have an abortion; you're too young."

Mr. Gumbel: "Instead she turns around and saves your life."

Mrs. Valencia: "Yeah and I think that's important; I think, you know, young girls today, even if you're pregnant, you know, think twice; this could save your life."

Now that's an interesting twist to the life-of-the-mother exception.[42]

---

42   World Magazine

7
ABORTION AND THE SANCTITY OF LIFE II

"He who frames the question usually wins the debate"
— Larry Tomczak

RESPONDING TO THE
15 MOST COMMON QUESTIONS[43]

Some say the time has come to abandon abortion as a vital issue because it is too divisive and other justice issues like poverty and protecting the environment help unify people. What must remain front and center is the reality that the sanctity of human life is the base upon which all justice issues rest.

We are called to "speak up for those who cannot speak for themselves,"[44] not compromise, and do so with winsomeness, clarity and gentle persuasion. Mahatma Gandhi, the primary influencer of Martin Luther King, Jr. said, *"Non-cooperation with evil is as much a duty as cooperation with good."*

To help you handle people's legitimate objections and questions, we provide you with the material:

1. *"Where do you stand on the abortion issue?"*

Because I believe in a Creator who gives us life and made us all in His image, my conviction is that every person has worth, dignity and value from conception 'til natural death. Our Founders affirmed that each person has a "right to life." Therefore, here are the two BIG questions: (1) "Is there such a thing as a life not worthy to be lived?" No. (2) "Would you take life 60 seconds before a person is born, or 60 seconds before that, or 60 seconds before that?" No to all because once life begins it is not our right to terminate what God miraculously began.

2. *"Isn't abortion merely 'terminating a pregnancy?'"*

---

43   World Magazine
44   Book of Proverbs, Chapter 31:8

There are two points to consider here. First, recognize the euphemism. We shouldn't just say that abortion "terminates a pregnancy" – abortion *takes the life of an unborn child*. The unborn child is a person, not an abstraction – a "product of conception."

Secondly, abortion does not merely "terminate a pregnancy." (Can you imagine headlines like this: "Lee Harvey Oswald Terminates Kennedy's Presidency!"?) At conception, the entire genetic code is present which determines what a person will look like as an adult; by the 18th day the heart has begun to beat; by the 30th day all major structures of the body are evident ("launched" for development).

3. *"Isn't this a political issue best left to politicians, judges, public opinion polls or states to decide?"*

This is primarily a *moral* issue for which we are all accountable. Judeo-Christian foundations in America have always upheld the sanctity of life and it is only since a Supreme Court decision in 1973 that abortion was considered legal throughout our land. Millions believe this was a tragic error, like prior decisions regarding black Americans, and want to see protection for the unborn restored.

4. *"What about politicians who say they are 'pro-life' but don't want to impose their personal views on other?"*

This clever attempt to "dodge the issue" is similar to someone saying they oppose sexual molestation of children and stalking by predators but don't want to impose their personal views on others.

5. *"Isn't abortion a safe, harmless procedure like other surgeries, say a root canal or tonsillectomy?"*

Absolutely not. It is an operation terminating the life of a developing baby. If it was simply like these two mentioned, why are there so many post-abortion support groups and scores of women getting professional counseling and grief therapy? Why do you think the majority of people choose not to even look at pictures of an abortion or the remains of the dismembered little baby? Have you spoken with or read testimonies of women with abortion-related physical and psychological problems that cause ongoing remorse and regret? This is a serious issue.

6. *"Should a candidate's position on abortion be a single issue 'litmus test' to qualify or disqualify him or her for election?"*

A single issue shouldn't qualify someone for office but a single issue can disqualify him. This must be examined since you can judge the character of a person by how he treats those who can do nothing for him. The dignity of human life is, in a sense, a thread that touches upon our life-connection with the poor, elderly, disabled, the prisoner, the AIDS patient, the sex slave or any of life's most vulnerable.

To the charge that we are "single-issue" voters, simply point out that there are numerous single issues that disqualify a person for office (someone endorsing rape, bribery, corporate fraud or bigotry). If we have laws forbidding cruelty to animals (ask Michael Vick if it is a crime to maim, mutilate or kill even an animal), why not the same concern for unborn babies? We don't vote for a candidate simply because they uphold the sanctity of life – they must be called and competent. Yet this reveals their moral fiber and ethics. *I personally have a conviction to never support a candidate who supports abortion!*

7. *"Is it love to bring unwanted children into the world where they will be neglected, abused, and poverty-stricken?"*

Just because a pregnancy is initially unwanted or unplanned does not necessarily mean that the baby will be unwanted when born. And should the biological parents not desire to care for their newborn, there are hundreds of thousands of couples (many who have waited up to seven years due to a shortage of available babies) who are eager to adopt.

Concerning poverty; are we to conclude that death is better than being poor? Jesus said, "The poor you will always have with you." But love never takes innocent human life; rather, love always seeks to heal, to help, and to extend constructive alternatives.

8. *"Is an unborn baby or fetus viable?"* (Viable: "able to live outside the womb")

First of all, remember what the term "fetus" means. It's Latin for "little one" or "offspring." We are talking about a developing human being. Now to say that a baby should not be guaranteed the right-to-life simply because he or she cannot survive outside the womb is unfair. Should we deny "preemies" the right to life because they cannot live without machine assistance? And should we deny the right-to-life to infants because they cannot survive without 24 hours-a-day supervision and care?

9. *"Doesn't a woman have the right to control her own body?"*

The baby is not just "part of the woman's body" like her liver or lungs. It is a totally separate person with 46 chromosomes, a separate blood system (often with totally different blood type) and its own unique body parts.

Beyond this it must be understood that no person has absolute rights over their own body. All of us are subject to certain civil laws which restrict our personal "rights." For example, a woman may not legally sell her body for prostitution; she may not legally inject narcotic drugs into her body; and she may not legally kill herself. In these ways she does not have a total "right" to control her own body. No one does.

10. *"Aren't you trying to impose your morality on everybody else?"*

There is an incorrect assumption here that nobody should attempt to impose their moral views upon anybody else. It ignores the obvious fact that laws "impose" morality upon others (e.g. it's illegal to steal, to cheat on your income tax, or to run naked through the shopping mall). The truth is that someone's morality determines the fate of the innocent unborn. God and our founding Fathers stated everyone has a "right to life."

11. *"But didn't the Supreme Court make abortion legal?"*

Yes. They also declared that black people were not citizens, but merely "property" in the Dred Scott decision of 1857. They were wrong then; and they are wrong again in their abortion decision of 1973. Just as courageous people took a stand then against an immoral law and won a victory for justice, so too in our day are we called to take a stand for the defenseless baby in the womb.

12. *"But didn't the Supreme Court make abortion legal?"*

Yes. They also declared that black people were not citizens, but merely "property" in the Dred Scott decision of 1857. They were wrong then; and they are wrong again in their abortion decision of 1973. Just as courageous people took a stand then against an immoral law and won a victory for justice, so too in our day are we called to take a stand for the defenseless baby in the womb.

13. *"What about the cases of rape, incest, and instances when the life of the mother is in danger?"*

First of all, two wrongs never make a right. To end a baby's life because of the wrong of someone else does nothing but compound an already difficult situation. What a woman needs when facing a crisis pregnancy is love and support, not an "easy out."

Secondly, when people focus attention on these extraordinary situations they neglect the fact that over 97% of all abortions have nothing to do with these crises. The overwhelming majority of abortions are performed strictly for personal convenience.

14. *"What about the cases where the child may be born handicapped or deformed?"*

Since when has it become a capital offense to be less-than-perfect? The assumption here is one which declares: "Children born with deformities or handicaps will not live a fully meaningful life. Theirs will be a miserable existence." No evidence supports this misguided viewpoint.

Consider the names of some who've suffered severe handicaps: Helen Keller (blind and deaf), Stevie Wonder (blind from birth), Franklin Delano Roosevelt (crippled from polio), Beethoven (deaf), Steven Hawking (genius) and Christopher Reeve (actor). Did they live non-meaningful lives?

15. *"Aren't the majority of Americans in favor of legal abortion?"*

No. This is an area where some distort statistics. They will proclaim that "only 16% of all Americans are opposed to a total ban on all abortion." However if the question is asked differently, such as: "Are you in favor of aborting unborn babies in all situations?" the statistics shift dramatically. Finally, just because the majority says so doesn't make it right. Remember the "majority" once said "Crucify Jesus Christ," and "Black people were 'property,' not persons!"

16. *"Do you want abortion forced to back-alleys where tens of thousands of women will once again die?"*

Former abortion-rights activist Dr. Bernard Nathanson admits that he and his co-founders of NARAL (National Abortion Rights Action League) fabricated the figure that a million women were getting illegal abortions in America yearly with tens of thousands dying. The doctor who is now pro-life and opposes abortion, states that the average was about 98,000 illegal abortions with an average of about 250 deaths for the 25 years before 1973. Plus, 90% of these were done in doctor's offices – not back alleys! And, yes, some died as they still do even in our day.

Should we legalize and sanction heroin addiction because some people die in back-alleys due to overdoses and dirty needles? Should we legalize and promote prostitution as a legitimate business in order to curb the spread of rape and venereal disease? And remember, the central issue is this: There is *another* human being whose life is at stake.

8

HOMOSEXUALITY AND THE FUTURE OF THE FAMILY I

-THE CORNERSTONE –

**"Love is justice – a charity,
Love brings with it a clarity."
— Bono/U2
Song "Mercy"**

G.I. JOE, BARBIE AND MR. POTATO HEAD

Growing up, most of us have memories of imaginative playtimes with a favorite doll or action-figure. Whether alone or with siblings and friends, you probably owned one of the two most popular figures of the past fifty years – G.I. Joe and Barbie.

If you were a guy, you and your buddies may have outfitted your soldier for battle and then proceeded to mow down opposing forces with a venom that may have brought the wrath of mom. "Will you boys quiet down! And do not, I repeat, DO NOT knock over any of my valuables."

If you were a girl, you may have gathered your gal pals for a pretend party while brushing out Barbie's life-like long blond hair. Glamour held sway as attractive outfits and jewelry were put in place at the tea party, eagerly awaiting the arrival of Mr. "Hubba Hubba" – Ken.

In all our years, most of us probably never came across a bunch of boys cooing and cuddling with Barbie while sipping their tea, any more than we ever witnessed a grouping of giggly girls slam-banging G.I. Joe across tanks to demolish the plastic soldiers standing in his way. (Okay. Okay.There's usually some rare exception. Someone out there in Boise, Idaho, can cite a time where Jimmy and Mickey were seen with our little princess, but are you sure they weren't priming her with firecrackers to blow off her pretty head once mom and sis weren't around?!).

Women Are from Venus, Men Are from Mars. That's the title of the best seller that stated the obvious – men and women are different. Studies bear this out. So does history and experience. Same with Scripture: "Male and female He created them."[45]

Now Mr. Potato Head was a different story. If you had one, both boys and girls often enjoyed the ingenious mischief of taking his plastic core body and sticking the various interchangeable body parts in places where they didn't belong. Remember squealing the same way you did when someone "passed gas" and got smacked upside the head for doing it in public? It seemed odd and out of order. It looked strange. Yet it was only poor ole' Mr. Potato Head with the ear jammed into the mouth slot, the arm jimmied where the leg belonged and the plastic lips stuck in that silly eye socket!

HERE'S THE DEAL…whether you cite "Mother Nature" or "Nature's God" (as our Founding Fathers did), men and women are designed and function differently, complement and complete each other, and through the wonder of marital union are able to procreate with each other to perpetuate the cycle of life. When things are in order, there's a beauty to this self-evident plan. When disregarded, things seem strange, kinda' like messing around with Mr. Potato Head.

One night on "Larry King Live," Rick Warren, author of the 30 million best seller *The Purpose Driven Life*, was asked about homosexual behavior. The down-to-earth, plain-and-simple response Rick gave the veteran interviewer left Larry a bit taken aback. "Just stand a naked man and a naked woman together and it's obvious how God designed us!"

Today confusion is abounding in areas of sexuality, marriage and family. Canada and some European nations have drifted from their Judeo-Christian foundations and acted contrary to thousands of years of historical precedent by endorsing homosexual activity and homosexual marriage. The roots are secular and the branches are extending our way under the guise of "progressive" thinking and "courageous" leadership.

---

45   Book of Genesis, Chapter 1:27

I KISSED A GIRL

"*I Kissed A Girl.* That's it – the number one song in America this week sung by the hot new artist, Katy Perry. Her new album features the groundbreaking hit, 'RU Gay?' It's now available in stores or download it at...."

'Cuse me! Did I hear what I thought I heard? This isn't a catchy tune for young people about "goin' surfin'" or "falling in love again," it's about the thrill of two girls locking lips! Medically it refers to two orbicularis orifice muscles in a state of contraction. Sexually it raises questions about the appropriateness of certain types of behavior between members of the same sex. And, oh yeah, the song targets the demographic group that is most impressionable – teens. Understandably, moms and dads across America are rattled by current cultural trends.

- Madonna and Britney engage in a full view, passionate kiss on the MTV awards telecast.

- Comedian Ellen DeGeneres and her live-in lover say, "That's amore!" and are totally open about their lesbian relationship (picked up after Ellen's former lover left her for another... man!). After all, lots' of Hollywood celebs – male and female – celebrate "coming out of the closet."

- Rapper, Lil Wayne, releases his new album and it sells a million copies its first week. Listeners get pounded with 'f'-words, drug pushing, murderous boasts ("Slit your throat/Have you smilin' through your neck"), oral sex and gang executions. And, oh yeah, women are called "bitches" by what many believe is in reality a raunchy thug.

- The 6:30pm "family fare," for us Nashvillians is Fox's animated cartoon, "Family Guy" and his "normal" suburban family. Viewers get hit with an average 20 profanities per episode as the beer-swilling, porn-loving doofus dad systematically breaks every taboo imaginable. Nudity...bestiality...sodomy...smoking... dope...genital jokes...rape... bulimia...animal cruelty...hey, it's all cartoon humor – great for training the kids.

Flip on any channel – network TV or cable – and a virtual potpourri of offerings emerge: "Weeds" has a suburban mom selling pot. "Breaking Bad" has suburban chemistry teachers making meth. "Big

Love" features suburban polygamists. CBS has suburban couples in mutual adultery – "Swingtown" to complement ABC's suburban gays and freewheelin' females on "Desperate Housewives."

Round out the picture with songs, films and "pop" publications promoting "anything goes" lifestyles, especially chic gay couples, gay lifestyles, gay marriage and gay adoption…. "C'mon," say some people, "What's the big deal?!"

Some respond: "Nothing. It's a mark of progressive people." Others recoil: "Everything. It's a sign of a society in decline." Multitudes of decent citizens are confused and because few of us want to be viewed as backwards and bigoted, we clam up yet deep down inside are extremely uncomfortable with what's happening regarding the coarsening of our culture. If you're a parent today, this has special relevance for you.

Specifically, WHAT DO *YOU* REALLY THINK ABOUT WHAT'S GOING ON?

Admittedly, there is a lot of confusion as we've drifted away from the truth. Remember the progression cited earlier, *rejecting truth* results in *loss of discernment* and ultimately *moral chaos*. Denial of truth undermines people's attempts to handle sexual issues as "every man does what is right in his own eyes." When natural order is disregarded, it leads to the downward spiral explained by the brilliant theologian, Paul, when he penned the following to the emerging church in Rome.

> *"The wrath of God (His righteous anger) is being revealed from heaven against all the godlessness and wickedness of men who suppress the truth (**REJECT TRUTH**) . . . although they knew God, they neither glorified Him as God nor gave Him thanks, but their thinking became futile and their foolish hearts were darkened (**LOSS OF DISCERNMENT**). . . . They exchanged the truth of God for a lie…. Because of this, God gave them over to...[what follows is a cascading list of behaviors including 'shameful acts, perversion, greed, deceit, envy, murder, strife, arrogance, dishonoring parents and inventing ways of doing evil' (**MORAL CONFUSION**)]."*

Although it's a difficult pill for some to swallow, the record stands: Homosexuality is not merely a harmless, "gay" lifestyle that folks are born into, it is the unmistakable consequence of rejecting truth about God and His plan for mankind. And when it says people "receive in their own bodies the due penalty for their sin," this explains why men engaging in this behavior become effeminate in speech and mannerisms while women become more mannish in appearance and behavior as well.

It is not stereotyping – it is straight talk.

This is not "hate speech" or "homophobia" – it's giving people hope that change is possible – if they want it.

CHARITY AND CLARITY

Because of individuals who, in the past and regrettably in the present, approach this issue in a mean-spirited, even hateful way, it is incumbent upon us to conduct ourselves as Bono sang in U2's song "Mercy," with utmost charity without compromising clarity.

An excellent role model here would be Jesus Christ who exemplified the two paramount qualities that are essential as we proceed. The hallmarks of his life were being "full of grace and truth."[46] Grace – full of love, compassion, mercy and genuine care. Truth – that which is true, right and full of integrity. Knowing the collapse of character begins on compromise corner, let's make a quality decision to not neglect either one.

It's been said, the head usher to happiness is a well-kept conscience. All of us have a conscience – which needs to be properly formed – and it is to the conscience we will speak in this chapter. This internal compass is akin to the "red light" on our dashboard. If it lights up and we punch it out – we do so to our peril. It's not there to annoy but rather to signify something is amiss under the hood. As we deal with this issue, all of us need to heed our consciences to ascertain if we've strayed from the proper path: Christ-like civility coupled with clear cut, truth-centered convictions.

Author, C.S. Lewis once said, "God whispers to us in our pleasures, speaks in our conscience, but shouts in our pains. It is his megaphone to rouse a deaf world." Today multitudes are experiencing whispers, statements and shouts to jolt us out of our slumber and into a greater awareness of what's actually going on around us.

Dr. Martin Luther King, Jr. said, "The church is neither the master of

---

46   Gospel of John, Chapter 1:17

the state, nor the servant of the state, but rather the conscience of the state." He knew the strength of a nation and its citizens stemmed from heeding a well-informed conscience.

Another Martin Luther (for whom the civil rights activist was named) championed the Protestant Reformation of the 16th century that shook the entire world. Refusing to back down even though his position in confronting corruption meant certain death, this German attorney and religious leader invoked his conscience in stating his case:

> *"Unless you prove to me by Scripture and plain reason that I am wrong, I cannot and will not recant. My conscience is captive to the Word of God. To go against conscience is neither right nor safe. It endangers the soul. Here I stand. There is nothing else I can do. God help me."*

He also stated these words which have relevance as we approach this topic:

> *"If I profess with the loudest voice and clearest exposition every portion of the truth of God except precisely that little point that the world and the devil are at the moment attacking,* I am not confessing Christ, *however boldly I may be professing Christ. Where the battle rages is where the loyalty of the soldier is proved, and to be steady on all the battlefield besides, is merely flight and disgrace if he flinches at that point."*

HERE'S THE DEAL: It's time for grace and truth to prevail as we look at homosexuality and gay marriage in America. The battlefield is the family and history bears out: As the family goes, so goes the nation. This all affects *you!*

BACK TO THE FUTURE

To gain clarity on this issue, it's helpful to return to the period of the 60's upheaval, for it was during these turbulent years that the "Gay Liberation" movement was launched. As restraints were being chucked overboard regarding drugs, sex, divorce, pornography, profanity, nudity, extra-marital affairs, living together and abortion, homosexuality had its place at the table.

Any one of the above areas could be likened to a broken window on a city street. One smashed window can be an invitation to another and another. If vandalism is left unchecked, a city can slowly but surely deteriorate. That may help you comprehend the moral freefall we're experiencing in America.

Since the turbulent era of the mid-60's, the state of marriage and the family has become very fragile, a reality with dire implications for our future. We've come a long way since French Statesman, Alexis de Tocqueville observed regarding our country, "There is certainly no country in the world where the tie of marriage is more respected than in America."

Nineteen sixty seven's "Summer of Love" and beyond have left lots of debris on our moral landscape. Without pointing fingers, all of us should engage in some candid reflection regarding what contribution we may have made to astronomical divorce rates, abortion, out-of-wedlock birthrates and spousal abuse. People of faith should lead the way in genuine humility and seeking forgiveness for whatever poor example we've provided and then re-order our lives to model the message multitudes need to hear.

A poet once said, "The mass of humanity live lives of quiet desperation." How true today. Consequences of the "Free lovin'" era are now so evident as scores are seeking sanity and solutions to their shattered lives, the gay community included.

Again, let's go 'back to the future' to comprehend what's happened.

In 1973, the American Psychiatric Association was persuaded to remove homosexuality from its list of psychiatric illnesses and reclassify it as "normal behavior." Homosexuality, a term describing same-sex involvement, was to be accepted, tolerated and characterized as "gay" – a carefree life of bliss, happiness, abounding in pleasure. From bathhouses in San Francisco to swinger's clubs in New York, the party seemed unending. Flaunting the "restrictive" mores of our nation's heritage and the Judeo-Christian foundations of Western Civilization, gays and lesbians were encouraged to "come out of the closet" and celebrate unrestrained sexual liberation.

Then, in the early 80's, a soft explosion was detonated – something beyond anyone's wildest imagination. What began as eerie rumors about some fellas getting low-grade fever, losing weight, developing some mysterious skin condition and then wasting away to skeletal proportions, gave way to the shocking reality of what the media initially labeled, "The Gay Plague." Buff, toned, young, healthy gay men and their multiple partners were gripped by fear. Who had it? Who'd be next? Most everyone in the gay community was scared. How could this have happened?

Infected gay men used and reused dirty needles from drug involvement and the "Gay Plague" spread to fellow gays and "straight" folks in America and abroad. Homosexual drug addicts used their needles and when prostitutes were added to the mix, AIDS mushroomed in ways unimaginable.

Outside of faithful, monogamous married couples, "sexually active" (the new term) gays and straights were infected at alarming rates and soon the words "epidemic" and "pandemic" appeared. Africa got hit hard as did other nations where sexual permissiveness was not restrained by religious or governmental influences.

Decades later I stood with my son at Harvard's commencement exercises as Justin graduated from "The Kennedy School of Government and Public Policy." Kofi Annan, Secretary General of the United Nations, spoke of the challenges the global community faced. Later in a column appearing in USA Today, he continued the ten-alarm, fire alert.

"In the 25 years since the first case was reported, AIDS has changed the world. It has killed 25 million people and infected 40 million more. It has become the world's leading cause of death among both women and men ages 15 to 59. It has inflicted the single greatest reversal in the history of human development. In other words, it has become the greatest challenge of our generation."

TIME FOR TRUE COMPASSION
AND TRUE TRUTH

The time has arrived for everyone involved in the public dialogue on homosexuality and gay marriage to lower our voices, approach one another with respect and demonstrate true compassion for those who are hurting. For those who are Christians, we need to remember our social responsibility and ramp up our care for those who are sick as the "least of these my brethren." (Imagine if we had done this at the onset of the AIDS epidemic how we could have alleviated suffering plus gained credibility as caring people of faith.)

Christ's disciples have a mandate to "overcome evil with good" and follow His example as a "friend" of the rejected and unloved. We need to extend the same acceptance and forgiveness given to us while protecting those maligned from the ridicule and attacks to which they've often been subjected.

When basketball superstar Magic Johnson came down with the HIV virus, he said these words: "I had my fun, but now I have to pay the price." Many who don't have the resources that Magic had, identified with his remorse but were not so "lucky" to stay alive. Others continue on the struggle but are probably in one of the following categories:

- Some gays say they are *militant* –Rough and ready to be combative with anyone perceived as opposing their radical agenda.

- Some gays call themselves *moderate* – Having found acceptance in a lifestyle they've discovered or with which they're experimenting, they see themselves on a journey – still trying to find ultimate peace or purpose in life.

- Some gays acknowledge they are *moving on* – Acknowledging the emptiness of a lifestyle they once thought would satisfy, they're abandoning it and asking for caring relationship and community to support them on their journey back to wholeness.

My window of opportunity came a while back with John who went from the second grouping to the third but unfortunately it was too late. True compassion for me (Larry) meant regular visits to a hospice for John, a former gay as he battled the ravages of AIDS. Just being there, listening, encouraging and reassuring him along with his precious, young daughter, meant the world to him. Later I was able to take care of his memorial service in a way that I trust inspired all of his former friends to reflect on his life and theirs.

Joe Dallas, once a homosexual and now the Program Director for the New Liberty Sexual Addiction Program had his chance to display compassion by overcoming evil with good as he shares in this experience.

I had the pleasure of speaking at a Promise Keepers men's conference a few years back. Gay militant groups were converging on the conference because they had heard that Promise Keepers had spoken out against homosexuality. They said, "We're going to come in and bust the place up. We're going to make sure you know we're there. We're not going to give you a chance to speak."

It so happened that year, some of the guys from the Denver Broncos were coming down to help with security. Well, we were secure. They stood around the outside of the stadium with arms locked. They were quiet, but impressive. These men were basically forming a boundary saying, "This is as far as it goes. You may come here. You may exercise your right to speech, but you will not disrupt what we're doing."

As the evening wore on, some of the guys thought maybe the demonstrators were getting hungry. A few of them broke ranks, went into the speaker's room, got some coffee and juice and cookies. Quite a sight – these guys hulking out into a bunch of gay demonstrators saying, "No, you're not going to disrupt our conference but do you want some cookies while you're out there?"[47]

This combination of charity and clarity is what's needed today. Doctor Martin Luther King, Jr. reminds us, "Whom you would change, you must first love."

Politicians must be especially careful to model charity without relinquishing clarity, as many are apt to do. Winston Churchill was certainly an example of uncompromising conviction yet at times he lacked the graciousness we can't afford to emulate. On one occasion he had this interchange with his chief British opponent.

LADY ASTOR: "If I were your wife, I would put poison in your coffee."

WINSTON: "And if I were your husband, I would drink it!"

Today the good news is that people of faith are responding to help homosexuals (and drug users, prostitutes and tragically the innocent children put at risk by AIDS). Pastor Rick Warren has been traveling to Africa and advocating for the victims of this disease. Franklin Graham and Samaritan's Purse held a conference, "Prescription for Hope," attended by close to 1,000 people from 86 countries in serving those

---

47   How Should We Respond? – Joe Dallas, Focus on the Family Organization

with AIDS. Ordinary Christians, Jews and others are awakening to compassionate ways of service. My own adopted daughter Renee recently devoted 5-1/2 months ministering to abandoned AIDS babies in Johannesburg, South Africa, where AIDS is out of control.

Charitable conduct and service is increasing and must be encouraged a hundred fold. Where we need to be careful is in our quest to do good we not relinquish our voice to help keep the conscience attuned as Dr. Martin King reminds us. Maintaining clarity along with the charity is a formidable task.

HERE'S THE DEAL: The predominant cause of the AIDS epidemic (where there are multitudes suffering as innocent victims) stems from destructive, behavioral choices. If we're forthright about the root of the problem, we then can help prevent its spread along with helping those in need.

Some politicians, pundits and experts say "Cool it on the spiritual and simply zero in on the physical side of this disease that presently takes the lives of 8,500 people every day." In other words, distribute condoms and clean needles (as well as other medical necessities) but don't talk about the morality aspect – that's "judgmental."

The C.D.C. (Center for Disease Control) is so desperate with the escalating situation we face it has actually resorted to giving out gift cards to entice gay and bisexual men to get HIV testing! Five million of our tax dollars was committed in 2008 for this five-year campaign.

"THE WISDOM WE NEED TO FIGHT AIDS"

New York Times columnist David Brooks wrote an article with the above title in June of 2005. Surprisingly, after his trip to Africa, he stated, "We have mostly tried technical means to prevent the spread of AIDS, and these techniques have proved necessary but insufficient." He went on to say that people don't honor "the sanctity of life"…"predatory men knowingly infect women by the score." He cited other examples of targeting evil and how positive change resulted. One husband, after he contracted HIV, stopped his promiscuous sex, drunkenness and spousal abuse and his wife now counsels others regarding the disease.

In other words, wisdom dictates *we minister to the ailing and helpless with every physical resource available but not ignore the reality that there is a spiritual dimension that has to be clearly confronted.* To ignore the moral aspect in AIDS prevention and believe drugs and condoms can save the day is to deny the truth and never get at the root of the problem – tainted human nature which needs to change. This is what Barack Obama stated in his Time magazine interview (August '08) where he spoke of the need for a "heart" change – not mere government policies.

The same logic applies to America's so-called "War on Drugs." Since 1973, this drug war has cost U.S. taxpayers (you and me!) over $500 billion dollars! Nearly 500,000 people are behind bars on drug charges today, yet drugs are as available as ever. While it's true we need to continue pouring more money into education, treatment and prevention, if we miss the root cause this problem only escalates.

"Wisdom cries aloud in the street, in the open squares she raises

Her voice…. How long, you simple ones, will you love simplicity,

How long will you turn away from my reproof?"[48]

THE TRUTH ABOUT HOMOSEXUALITY

HERE'S THE DEAL: Because we are committed to both charity and clarity in dealing with this issue (not just AIDS but the entirety of homosexual activity), we must lovingly and honestly lay it on the line. To say we genuinely care about our fellow man, yet not "speak the truth in love" is, pardon the expression, preposterous B.S.

A few years ago I noticed a red lesion on my back that my wife encouraged me to check out with a dermatologist. He assessed it as "pre-cancerous" and subsequently removed it by burning it off my back (Ow!). The ingredients:

Time invested; honest assessment; pain experienced; affliction eradicated; health restored.

Would the doctor have been a true healer and friend if he sidestepped the root problem out of fear that he'd offend me and instead merely applied a bandage to my sore, sending me on my way? I could be dead today from his nicety minus the necessity of truth-telling!

Now, we grant you, compassionately conveying truth doesn't

---

48   Book of Proverbs, Chapter 1:20-21

guarantee someone will act upon the truth. Each person has been born with a propensity to do wrong and has a free will to resist or yield.

Take, for instance, the atheistic father of modern psychiatry – Sigmund Freud. He pioneered much of what we hear today: "Let go of inhibitions. Stop repressing your sex drives. Get in touch with the real you and let yourself go."

On September 21, 1939, Sigmund Freud took the hand of the physician at his bedside and said, "My dear Schur, you promised not to forsake me when my time comes. Now it is nothing but torture and makes no sense anymore."

Of what was he dying?

Years before, Sigmund's doctor listened to his irregular heartbeat and counseled him to stop his cigar smoking. Dr. Freud stopped for a short time, but decided to resume the habit.

He subsequently suffered through thirty-five operations for cancer of the jaw, finally losing his entire lower jaw and resembling a bit the grotesque "split-faced" villain in Batman. Physicians warned him repeatedly that he was risking his life by continuing to smoke, but he refused to heed them. The tobacco habit consumed him and he eventually died.

Dr. Freud could analyze the human mind. He could diagnose problems. But in reality couldn't or wouldn't change.

For the record, people do have the "freedom" to somewhat do as they please – within certain limits. No persons have unrestricted liberty to do anything they want – especially if it's harmful to themselves or others. People cannot yell "fire" in a theatre, carry a gun on a plane, run naked through the mall or cruise through a neighborhood seventy miles an hour while polishing off a 6 pack of Colt 45.

Likewise, individuals are free to engage in private homosexual conduct, but tens of millions of decent Americans along with our children and parents do not have to be exposed to it. Neither does a government have to legitimize it by sanctioning it in official ways (like gay marriage). There's a big difference between allowing something and endorsing it.

Bottom line: Homosexual activity is morally wrong – just as adultery

– but that does not necessarily translate into it being outlawed. It simply should not be officially endorsed by a government representing us or given a seal of approval to convey mainstream respectability.

TOP THREE QUESTIONS

Debunking the Myths and Misconceptions
Delivering the Facts and Truth

1. *Is homosexuality a sin forbidden by God?*

Absolutely. We're aware this is contrary to what some "religious," "gay affirming" churches and leaders put forth (they reject the authority of the Bible and twist the meaning of passages), but they must be challenged and called back to faithfulness to the truth. The Bible consistently, unambiguously, without exception prohibits homosexuality, and tells us to honor God's design for sexual behavior between men and women.[49] The purpose is that we enjoy a fulfilling sexual experience in marriage and ideally have children as an expression of our marital love. Stating this forthrightly is not "hate speech" any more than warning someone they're about to walk off a cliff is "hate speech." This is an expression of divine love because sinful behavior not only hurts our Creator but is harmful to us (and others). God gives us laws for our own good!

Laws are essential in every area of life in order to maintain order and harmony. In the area of our *physical* body there are many rules. We human beings must eat wisely or problems surface. (Ever see the film "Super Size Me?!") It's the same thing with getting proper rest.

In the *mental and emotional* realms one must follow rules to become stable and mature. A person who is self-centered, increasingly fearful of people, distrusts himself and lives in isolated anxiety can end up goin' bananas and placed in a mental institution.

In *sports*, there's always a book of rules with "instant replays" insuring they are kept. Imagine the mess if everyone decided to "do their thing" in a baseball game – the batter steps up holding a tennis racket instead of a bat; the pitcher stands on first base and throws footballs; five guys huddle together in right field holding hockey sticks while bowling balls are slam-dunked in sideline hoops.

---

49   Passages from the Holy Bible: Gen. 19:4-7, Judges 19:22-23, Lev. 18:22, 29-30, Lev. 20:13, Deut. 22:5, I Cor. 6:9-11, Rom. 1:24-28, 32, I Tim. 1:9-10, Jude 7.

In **society**, we have laws against stealing, murder, adultery. Without them we'd degenerate into anarchy, a "dog-eat-dog" jungle. Wherever we turn in life we are confronted by laws – rules and regulations. The key is to see them as our friends and not our enemies.

I know a girl who purchased a microwave oven and didn't bother to read the instructions – the rules of operation. Late for an appointment, she quickly put her poodle in the oven to dry him off after a bath while she finished blow-drying her hair. You guessed it! But, after all, who needs "rules?"

Think of it, this way when it comes to the human sexual experience, Sex is like a can of Drano – a great product. *But if it is not used according to directions, it can blow up right in your face!"*

During the Russian Revolution, an attempt was made to eliminate the biblical blueprint for sex and marriage. Legal restraints were taken off the books. Premarital sex, rather than being condemned, was given sanction by the state. Homosexual conduct, however, was not allowed.

The results? These decrees were so ruinous that in a relatively short time the government realized the strength of the nation was being destroyed. Therefore it issued a statement declaring that the state could not exist as it was going, and that chastity before marriage as well as fidelity in marriage was to be upheld, inasmuch as it was highly beneficial to the state.

Atheistic Russia – even while denying the existence of God – returned to sexual standards from scripture. Moral laws cannot be broken without devastating consequences. It may not be immediately, but it will be eventually. After the "kick" comes the kickback!

HERE'S THE DEAL: It's almost a no-brainer if a person wants to have a healthy and long life, honor divine standards and natural order regarding sexuality. Call it "street smarts" or "practical intelligence." Maybe it's just common sense.

Ask New York Governor, Eliot Spitzer, who resigned in disgrace (after adulterous activity with a prostitute) if he now regrets flaunting time-honored sexual standards intended to safeguard marriage and family. He probably wishes he had reached for the Gideon Bible in that posh D.C. hotel room rather than the attractive call girl. There he would have read:

- "For a prostitute is a deep pit and a wayward wife is a narrow well. Like a bandit she lies in wait, and multiplies the unfaithful among men."[50]

- "For the lips of an adulterous drip honey, and her speech is smoother than oil; but in the end she is bitter as gall, sharp as a double-edged sword. Her feet go down to death; her steps lead straight to the grave."[51]

Ask his wife and 3 daughters how they feel about what some "free-wheeling'" folks say about prostitution as a "victimless" vice. Contrary to glamorous images portrayed in the media like Julia Roberts in Pretty Woman, studies show 2/3 of prostitutes have been sexually abused as girls, a majority have drug dependencies, and almost ½ have attempted suicide (the mortality rate is 51 times that of the next most dangerous occupation for women).[52] It really is "practical intelligence" when we uphold the moral standards that are there for our good.

Or how about all the sexual experimentation triggered by the "Summer of Love" era of the mid-60's. Where has it gotten us as Americans? Consider what the C.D.C. released in 2008:

- More than 65 million live with an incurable STD.

- Each year Americans experience 19 million sexually transmitted diseases.

- Annually the explosion of HIV cases is actually 40 times higher than originally reported for the past decade.

- "1 in 4 girls between 14 and 19 is infected with at least one STD, and 48% of black girls now have an STD.

These alarming statistics are even worse because HIV/AIDs, syphilis and gonorrhea weren't included in the study!

The significance of these figures can't be overstated as STDs also cause infertility and cervical cancer. Isn't it basically "enlightened self-interest" to abide by the rules? It's not rocket science!

The genius, Albert Einstein, understood practical intelligence. He once said, "When I was young, I found out the big toe regularly ends up making a hole in a sock. So I stopped wearing socks!"

---

50   Book of Proverbs, Chapter 23:27-28
51   Book of Proverbs, Chapter 5:3-5
52   The American Journal of Epidemiology

Two boys were walking in a forest when they saw in the distance a ferocious grizzly bear charging towards them. One of the boys was considered smart by his teachers, the other of marginal intelligence.

The "smart" fella calculated real quick that the bear would overtake them in 37.5 seconds and they had no chance for escape. The second boy quickly laced up his jogging shoes.

"You gotta' be crazy," the first boy exclaimed. "There is no way we are going to outrun a grizzly bear!"

"That's true," replied the second boy, "but all I have to do is outrun you!"

That's practical intelligence – the ability to use your "smarts" to achieve success in life (or, in this case, a life-or-death experience).

How tragic to watch celebrities like dancer Rudolph Nureyov, Queen singer Freddie Mercury, an MTV "Real World" heart throb or countless others go down the "broad road" to ruin and death. Pop star George Michael revealed his "last remaining secret" (his homosexuality) after enduring an arrest for lewd behavior, the AIDS-related death of his "lover," drugs and finally severe depression on his self-destructive path. Genuine compassion should motivate us, as a former president said, "to feel their pain."

Even some gay activists are admitting the dangers of their risky behavior and the need to stop those who are reckless. Well-known gay leader Larry Kramer, himself HIV positive, spoke bluntly to gays: "You are still murdering each other! Stop all the generalizations and avoidance excuses...to ditch responsibility for this fact." And Richard Dohen, columnist and cheerleader for gay causes declared, "When you're victims of your own behavior, you need to be condemned!"

Why invite the health risks of homosexuality?

- The 2008 International Conference on AIDS in Mexico City reported: "Gay and bisexual men are 19 times more likely to become infected with AIDS than the general adult population (data collected from 128 nations)."

- Federal officials in 2008 acknowledged they have been underestimating the number of new AIDS infections in the U.S. by 40% every year for more than a decade!

- The CDC reported in August of 2008, 456,000 new cases of the HIV virus. The "majority are among homosexuals and bisexuals."

- STDs such as syphilis, HPV, gonorrhea and Chlamydia are rampant in the gay community (and continuing to increase among "sexually active" heterosexuals).

- Homosexuals experience appreciably higher rates of psychiatric illnesses, including depression, drug abuse and suicide attempts.

- Gays have shorter life spans – up to 20 years less!

- Gays also have alarming levels of sexually-related diseases such as anal and penile cancer.

- Half of AIDS patients appear to be stopping their medication or failing to begin treatment because of disfiguring side effects and clogged arteries. "The epidemic is – and has been – worse than was previously known," says Kevin Fenton of the U.S. Centers for Disease Control and Prevention.

When our family used to travel in our ole' Dodge mini-van for trips through Pennsylvania, there were numerous, long tunnels we'd go through, burrowed deep in the mountains. We'd all hold our breath (except the driver) to see who could "hold out" the longest. Going through those tunnels was a bit frightening at times. They were so dark, stark and musty. Yet all of us knew eventually they'd end and we could all breathe a sigh of relief as we expelled our pent-up breath, coming out into the light.

Sometimes in life we have to be willing to go through some dark tunnels of "truth telling" – uncomfortable and unpleasant as they are – to emerge into the light of day. Many believe a new day is dawning in the relationship between homosexuals and those who genuinely care enough to speak the truth in love about a lifestyle that is both immoral and harmful. (This is why in 86 nations of the world homosexual sex is considered a crime, and in seven countries it is punishable by death, according to the Foundation for AIDS Research known as AMFAR.)

Bono encouraged us to practice charity and clarity in our quest for greater justice in our world.

I trust we just did.

Question number two:

2. *"Is Homosexuality Simply Another Alternative Lifestyle – No Big Deal?"*

In the Hebrew-Christian Bible there are multiple times in both the Old and New Testament accounts where homosexual and other immoral activities are explicitly condemned as dishonorable to God and natural order (the way things were designed to work) and destructive to those involved with them. An entire chapter in the Old Testament[53] lists certain activities and calls them "detestable," stating in no uncertain terms: "Stay away!" In the New Testament it uses five terms to describe both male and female homosexual conduct as "unnatural," "perverted," "degrading," "shameful" and "indecent."[54] Not to be facetious, but is that hard to understand? Does that sound like "no big deal?"

Scripture forbids us to be sexually involved in seven areas: 1. Parents, 2. Children, 3. Brothers and sisters, 4. Another spouse, 5. Animals, 6. Dead people, 7. Same sex. These will never change.

Stated succinctly, the 3 basic reasons we are not to accept homosexuality as simply another normal, alternative lifestyle are as follows:

1. **Scriptural – no ambiguity**

2. **Anatomical – no possibility**

3. **Logical – no reproductivity**

Let's break these down –

We do want to warn you at this point that this next section needs to be labeled with a **PARENTAL ADVISORY ALERT**. We know that "it is a shame to speak of the things they do in secret,"[55] but we've reached the point as a nation where we must peel back the romanticized image of what goes on "behind the scenes" and come to grips with reality. Multitudes are blissfully ignorant and have been lulled to sleep by terms like "sexual orientation," "safe sex" and "human rights." They mistakenly view homosexual activity as a valid yet probably slightly different expression of normal human sexuality. What follows is slightly graphic, not suitable for children and admittedly disturbing.

HERE'S THE DEAL: What is happening to our country is equally disturbing.

---

53   Book of Leviticus, Chapter 18
54   Book of Romans, Chapter 1
55   Book of Ephesians, Chapter 5:12

It is not enough to simply say, "My sexual orientation is such-and-such, and everyone has a right to do as he pleases."

Stop a second and carry that premise to its logical conclusion. If we deviate from the natural order to say sexual orientation is whatever one wants, how do we deal with those who say, "My sexual orientation is not towards the opposite sex, but towards children…towards animals…toward dead people…towards whatever." Obliterating the natural design leaves off all these as morally equivalent.

Is this really what we want? The irreverent approach of now deceased comedian, George Carlin once said, "Find out where the line is drawn and cross it deliberately." This is not healthy for a society.

Already there are folks pushing to restore polygamy; folks pushing to allow "man-boy sexual relationships" (ever heard of NAMBA – National Assoc. of Man-Boy Alliance); or how about people with animals. In Phoenix, Arizona, where I've been about twenty times on my lifetime, the sheriff of Maricopa County, Joe Arpaio, wrote the following:

> *"Bestiality, an unsavory topic that had to be addressed." It seems that bestiality is a problem in Maricopa County: 'a public servant was caught by a young girl and her father in the act of attempting to engage in a sex act with the little girl's young lamb…. Recently a man was sexually abusing four dogs.'*[56]

The first reason we cannot accept homosexuality as simply another alternative lifestyle is that it is not scriptural. Let's be real specific.

SCRIPTURAL – NO AMBIGUITY

- "Before they had gone to bed, all the men from every part of the city of Sodom—both young and old—surrounded the house. They called to Lot, 'Where are the men who came to you tonight? Bring them out to us so that we can have sex with them.'"

  Lot went outside to meet them and shut the door behind him and said, 'No, my friends. Don't do this wicked thing.'"[57]

- "While they were enjoying themselves, some of the wicked men of the city surrounded the house. Pounding on the door, they shouted to the old man who owned the house, 'Bring out

56   Deer Valley Magazine, June '06.
57   Book of Genesis, Chapter 19:4-7

the man who came to your house so we can have sex with him.' The owner of the house went outside and said to them, 'No, my friends, don't be so vile. Since this man is my guest, don't do this disgraceful thing.'"[58]

- "Do not lie with a man as one lies with a woman; that is detestable.... 'Everyone who does any of these detestable things – such persons must be cut off from their people. Keep my requirements and do not follow any of the detestable customs that were practiced before you came and do not defile yourselves with them. I am the Lord your God.'"[59]

- "If a man lies with a man as one lies with a woman, both of them have done what is detestable. They must be put to death; their blood will be on their own heads."[60]

- "A woman must not wear men's clothing, nor a man wear women's clothing, for the Lord your God detests anyone who does this."[61]

- "Do you not know that the wicked will not inherit the kingdom of God? Do not be deceived: Neither the sexually immoral nor idolaters nor adulterers nor male prostitutes nor homosexual offenders nor thieves nor the greedy nor drunkards nor slanderers nor swindlers will inherit the kingdom of God. And that is what some of you were. But you were washed, you were sanctified, you were justified in the name of the Lord Jesus Christ and by the Spirit of our God."[62]

- "Therefore God gave them over in the sinful desires of their hearts to sexual impurity for the degrading of their bodies with one another. They exchanged the truth of God for a lie, and worshiped and served created things rather than the Creator – who is forever praised. Amen. Because of this, God gave them over to shameful lusts. Even their women exchanged natural relations for unnatural ones. In the same way the men also abandoned natural relations with women and were inflamed with lust for one another. Men committed indecent acts with other men, and received in themselves the due penalty for their perversion.

  "Furthermore, since they did not think it worthwhile to retain the knowledge of God He gave them over to a depraved mind, to do what ought not to be done."

---

58   Book of Judges, Chapter 19:22-23.
59   Book of Leviticus, Chapter 18:22, 29-30
60   Book of Leviticus, Chapter 20:13
61   Book of Deuteronomy, Chapter 22:5
62   Book of I Corinthians, Chapter 6:9-11

"Although they know God's righteous decree that those who do such things deserve death, they not only continue to do these very things but also approve of those who practice them."[63]

- "We also know that law is made not for the righteous but for lawbreakers and rebels, and ungodly and sinful, the unholy and irreligious; for those who kill their fathers or mothers, for murderers, for adulterers and the depraved, for slave traders and liars and perjurers – and for whatever else is contrary to the sound doctrine...."[64]

- "In a similar way, Sodom and Gomorah and the surrounding towns gave themselves up to sexual immorality and perversion. They serve as an example of those who suffer the punishment of eternal fire."[65]

The second and third reason we cannot accept homosexuality as simply another alternative lifestyle are as follows:

ANATOMICAL – NO POSSIBILITY
LOGICAL – NO REPRODUCTIVITY

Men and women were designed for each other. This is called natural order or creation/intelligent design. Sexual involvement in marriage brings pleasure as well as the possibility of children. Children aren't born any other way. The marital bond is to ensure stability and provision as the offspring grow. This simply is the way it works!

As *The Purpose Driven Life* book was a literary phenomenon selling over

30 million copies because people want to learn their purpose in life, so too is it imperative that we remind ourselves of the purpose of our sexual abilities.

"Do you know?"

HERE'S THE DEAL: The primary **PURPOSE** of our sexual abilities as designed is:

---

63   Book of Romans, Chapter 1:24-28, 32
64   Book of I Timothy, Chapter 1:9-10
65   Book of Jude, Verse 7.

1.   ONENESS (intimacy/bonding)

2.   OFFSPRING (procreation/children)

"Where's pleasure?!"

The **RESULT** of our sexual abilities is pleasure. It's critical we don't get all of this confused.

Here's some analogies:

- GOING TO THE BATHROOM – the *PURPOSE* is waste removal or cleansing of our system. The *RESULT* (depending on how bad you "gotta go") is relief or that feeling of "Ahhh."

- EATING A MEAL – the *PURPOSE* is nourishment and (remember the BeeGees, "Stayin' Alive"). The *RESULT* is enjoyment or pleasure.

When people bypass the purpose of something and mistakenly put the result in its place, things get out of alignment – just like our car or missing the first button on a shirt throws everything else off.

Natural order has men and women coupled together in marriage for the dual purpose of oneness and offspring. Same-sex unions cannot fully deliver on these two, so we're left with the element of pleasure alone. This may or may not last for long, which explains why there are so many multiple partnerships in the gay experience (as well as promiscuity and high incidences of AIDS/HIV/STDs).

Remember your Tinker toys as a child? They fit together.

As a high school student I (Larry) worked for an audio-visual firm and assembled devices that had a "male" plug and a "female" plug. The appropriate part had to be compatible with the other for things to work.

Because homosexuality is contrary to natural order, those who practice it have to force body parts into bodily openings that were designed for completely different functions. Put bluntly but necessarily unkindly, it "perverts" the natural order of things. Homosexual acts aren't marital intercourse – they are masturbation with another same-sex body.

The entire animal kingdom functions the same way in accordance with nature's design. Remember the "birds and the bees?" While some folks point to *rare* exceptions where some animals may dabble in homosexual-like activity, keep in mind they are animals operating out of instinct – not human beings operating out of reason and intellect.

Because homosexual acts are out of sync with the created order, they are not just unnatural – they are harmful. To compensate for what is missing, participants engage in various sexual practices including, but not exclusive to, the following:

[SECOND PARENTAL ADVISORY ALERT]

- Anal intercourse
- Oral sexual activity
- Fisting – the act of shoving one's fist….
- Rimming – the practice of licking orifices
- Golden Showering – urinating on partners
- Sex orgies – activities with groups of same-sex participants
- Anonymous sex – using openings in sex club cubicles for activity with strangers
- Sadomasochism –whippings, beatings, cuttings and beyond
- Drug parties – use of amphetamines, "coke" (not the soft drink) and ecstasy to enhance experiences like those listed here
- Mutual pleasuring and punishing
- Other "kinky," deviant practices.

Nationally known lesbian author, Camille Paglia once said, "History shows that male homosexuality, which like prostitution flourishes with urbanization and soon becomes predictably ritualized, always tends towards decadence – they are harmful."

Why do you think many homosexuals suffer immensely from what is medically known as "gay bowel syndrome?" Or the outbreak of herpes lesions in the mouth?

The spiritual, emotional, mental and physical well-being of homosexuals should be every decent American's concern. When behavior such as the above is engaged in, it is not simply "another alternative lifestyle" that is normal, acceptable and natural as many naively believe. As you've just read, it's not just same-sex couples hugging or pecking each other on the cheek!

The health costs related to AIDS and STD treatment are skyrocketing. The alarming levels of AIDS, STDs, suicides, depression, psychiatric illnesses and shorter life spans (at least 20 years among gay men and women) will not be solved by "safe sex" techniques and new medications.

HERE'S THE DEAL…it's time to recognize that many in our midst have been ignorant or desensitized to the strange and unnatural practices of homosexual men and women. While it's right to downplay the imagery, we can't give a little "wink and a nod" anymore and let this upcoming generation think "it's no big deal." Charity and clarity must undergird all we do.

Many parents today are very concerned about what their children are being taught about this issue in our schools. The 2.7 million-member National Education Association (N.E.A.) is promoting "gay-friendly" workshops to "educate" our children regarding gay, lesbian, trans-gender and bisexual issues. Many would be surprised and shocked at what's being put forth.

Where I formerly lived in Montgomery County, Maryland, a new sex-education curriculum for middle and high schools was stopped "minutes before midnight" due to the alertness of a mother named Laura Quigley. Children were about to learn that sex-play between same-sex adolescents is normal; teens should always wear condoms when engaging in vaginal, oral or anal sex, and that homosexuality was *not* a choice. As a concerned parent, Quigley had to go to court to finally put a stop to the program.

I include the following two letters that I trust illustrate how we can be charitable yet learn to speak up for decency in our day.

The first letter is one I wrote to the Atlanta president of The Kroger Corporation regarding their company's perceived support of an Atlanta "Gay Pride" event. I'm happy to report that Mr. Lucia's office responded immediately, apologized, acknowledged it was done "without his knowledge" and assured me it would not happen again.

Here's an excerpt from my letter:

Last night I went with a group of mature people from our church to the Gay Pride "Celebration" in Atlanta. We went to reach out with compassion and sensitivity to interested people at the event. Having counseled homosexual and lesbian folks, as well as having ministered to those with AIDS and sexually transmitted diseases, and having served in these ways for over 30 years, enables me to bring some experience "to the table."

As I walked through the audience I saw heavy drinking of alcohol, drugs, nudity, t-shirts with vulgarities, bare-breasted women, lewd conduct and, most of all, sadness and loneliness. If you were there with your wife, I wonder if you'd have similar observations. In addition, scores come from abused backgrounds, broken homes and very unfortunate childhood experiences. I genuinely love these men and women and can understand how many got to where they are today.

In a few minutes, I am departing for a hospice visit to a lady dying of liver cancer. The last time I went to a hospice I ministered to a young man (30) dying of AIDS who had turned away from his gay, promiscuous lifestyle – unfortunately too late.

Bruce, I write to tell you my wife and I are seriously contemplating not shopping at Kroger again after seeing the gay "Southern Voice" tabloid featuring a full page back cover ad from Kroger's saying you "Proudly Sponsor" this Gay Pride event. Unless I hear from you, I will assume your company is endorsing this lifestyle and I must withdraw support plus tell any others to consider this statement as well. Please ponder what I've said. Thank you, Larry T....

Note: Days after sending this letter I received a phone call from Mr. Lucia's personal assistant apologizing for what happened, citing it as a complete oversight. Although Bruce didn't know how this happened, I was reassured that it would not happen again.

Finally, here is a letter from a longstanding friend Michael L. Brown (a PhD teacher) to the Charlotte Observer newspaper in reference to their Charlotte "Gay Pride" gathering. Notice his articulate yet compassionate approach as he lifts the veil for people in his area to understand what many are simply unaware of today.

Here's an excerpt of his letter:

Charlotte Pride or Charlotte Shame?

Referring to the recent $195-a-plate gay dinner in the city, homosexual activist Shane Windmeyer stated that the event "offers an opportunity for us to come together and look at how we want Charlotte to be in five or 10 years."

What exactly does this mean? Does it mean more of what was flaunted at last May's "Charlotte Pride" event – more gay and lesbian couples passionately kissing in our public parks, more photos of totally naked men advertising "hot nudist camps," more overt references to little girls as "dikes on trikes"? (All this – and more – took place in Marshall Park last May.) Is this what Charlotte will look like in five or 10 years?

Perhaps it is time for a different agenda to be articulated, one that says, "We too have a vision for how this city will look in five or 10 years. And in our vision, what is now called Charlotte Pride will be remembered instead as Charlotte Shame."

I realize, of course, that even to hint at such things is to be immediately characterized as yet another religious homophobe. But should the fear of being caricatured stop one from speaking the truth? And isn't it ironic that those who most loudly call for tolerance are often the very ones who seek to suppress and muzzle all opposing views? Is not this the height of intolerance?

If it is acceptable for gays and lesbians to set forth their goals, why shouldn't it be acceptable for those holding to biblical values to set forth their goals as well? Or have those who hold to Judeo-Christian principles lost their right to speak?

Perhaps now that the gay agenda for this city has been announced and pursued, a positive agenda for morally-based cultural transformation can be announced and pursued. Perhaps it is now time even to ask our gay and lesbian friends – people whom we love and care for, but people whose agenda we oppose – Are you really proud of everything that took place at last year's "Pride" event? Is this how you want to be known? Surely, if traditional couples came together for a "Celebration of Marriage" day in a public park, little children would feel welcome, and people would not have to close their eyes and cover their ears to avoid contact with vulgar and obscene images, gestures, and words. Yet large homosexual celebrations worldwide are commonly marked by nude parades, men dressed in drag, open sex acts, and large signs proclaiming "God is gay." Is this what is next for Charlotte?

The third of our "Top Three Questions" is….

3. *"Are people born homosexual?"*

Earlier we stated something that bears repeating.

Admittedly, there is a lot of confusion as we've drifted away from the truth. Remember the progression cited earlier, rejecting truth results in loss of discernment and ultimately moral chaos. Denial of the truth undermines people's attempts to handle sexual issues as "every man does what is right in his own eyes." When natural order (God's design) is disregarded, it leads to the downward spiral explained by the brilliant thinker, Paul, when he penned the following to the emerging church in Rome.

"Therefore God gave them over in the sinful desires of their hearts to sexual impurity for the degrading of their bodies with one another. They exchanged the truth of God for a lie, and worshiped and served created things rather than the Creator— who is forever praised. Amen.

"Because of this, God gave them over to shameful lusts. Even their women exchanged natural relations for unnatural ones. In the same way the men also abandoned natural relations with women and were inflamed with lust for one another. Men committed indecent acts with other men, and received in themselves the due penalty for their perversion."[66]

Like it or not, the record stands: Homosexuality is not merely a harmless, "gay" lifestyle that folks are born into, it is the unmistakable consequence of rejecting truth about God and His plan for mankind. And when it says people "receive in their own bodies the due penalty for their sin," this explains why men engaging in this behavior become effeminate in speech and mannerisms while women become more mannish in appearance and behavior as well. It is not stereotyping – it's straight talk.

---

66   Book of Romans, Chapter 1:24-27 (NIV)

This is not "hate speech" or "homophobia" – it's giving people hope that change is possible – if they want it.

HERE'S THE DEAL: If we don't accept the truth about ourselves as revealed by the One who designed us, we're left to whatever explanation folks offer. If you have an invention, there has to be an inventor (did your cell phone simply fall into place?!) If you have a design, there has to be a designer. Let's be honest, Mount Rushmore with its sculpture of four famous Presidents on a huge granite cliff didn't just happen – someone (namely Sculptor, Gutzon Borglum) did it over fourteen years.

Recently I read an interview with a famous feminist who gained icon status for her song "I am Woman" – the anthem for the women's liberation movement of the 60's and 70's. Helen Reddy is now 66, alone, living in a rented 13th floor apartment and afraid she might not be able to pay the rent. In addition to speaking at chapters of N.O.W. (the National Organization for Women) she shares her "ideas" about how we got here. She attributes things to past-life regression and hypnotherapy.

As for her "past lives," Reddy

"believes she has lived hundreds, including one as an Egyptian foreman who worked on the Great Pyramids and another as a Persian merchant with multiple wives and concubines – a life that led her to have sympathy for women.

She also suspects she may have written the French national anthem during the French Revolution: "That would be two times in my life that I'd written an anthem!"[67]

In "I am Woman" she once boasted, "I am strong. I am invincible." In reading her comments I'd submit respectfully that she change the title of her song from "I am Woman" to "I am Confused Woman."

In answering the question, "Are People Born Homosexuals?" we go back to true truth. The answer is simple, No. Regardless of what so-called experts scientists and even religious scholars try to postulate, there is not a "gay gene" or inherited condition "causing" people to be born homosexuals and thereby lifelong victims to its pull. Furthermore, if homosexuality was inherited, it would tend to be eliminated from the human gene pool because those who supposedly "have it" don't reproduce!

---

67   USA Today, 4/17/08.

At the outset it is important to remind ourselves that homosexuality is a complex issue and we need to steer clear of stereotypes, sarcasm and superficial answers. Everyone in the public discussion must avoid any bashing, discrediting and name-calling ("Bigots…homophobes… NAZI's"), which is a divisive, manipulative tactic similar to when a certain company touts their "minty-green mouthwash as not being like those old, medicine-breath types."

While remaining charitable, there still must be no flip-flopping because this behavior is morally wrong (like adultery). Yet the good news is clear: There is hope and help for those seeking freedom! That said, we must be clear regarding the "biological determinism" argument or else a door is opened to justify any conduct like pedophilia, bestiality or rape by simply excusing oneself: "My genes made me do it."

"Is homosexuality okay if someone is in a 'loving, committed relationship?"

Stated simply - no. Throughout scripture, God's loving commandments, given for His glory and our good, prohibit the sexual *act* not just the attitude of the offender.

Now let's walk through this carefully.

- *ACCORDING TO SCRIPTURE AND SCIENCE, HOMO-SEXUALITY IS NOT PART OF SOMEONE'S BIOLOGICAL CONSTITUTION.*

It is not like "left handedness." There is absolutely no scientific evidence of a "gay gene" (two attempted studies regarding "twins" and "AIDS" both failed to prove anything, although some have tried to mislead people by citing them). Nature or Nurture? The answer is the latter. This is not opinion – its fact. Let's blow away the smoke from the smokescreen once and for all.

- *ALL OF US ARE BORN WITH A FALLEN NATURE THAT GIVES US A TENDENCY TO DO WRONG.*

We don't have to train children to lie, steal, harm others, act selfishly or demand their own way. Having a free will to make choices, all of us are accountable for our own actions. Biology can't make us do wrong, although circumstances can influence us. To say otherwise leaves people as victims, not responsible for their behavior.

- *THERE IS A MAJOR DISTINCTION BETWEEN PEOPLE'S BEHAVIOR AND PEOPLE'S RACE.*

One is chosen – the other unchosen. **Homosexuality is something someone does – not something someone is.** Each of us is personally responsible for our behavior (otherwise drunk drivers, rapists and child molesters are "off the hook," to play the "victim card"). To confuse this wrongly creates a new "minority" status and special "rights" for a very small segment of the population representing no more than 1 to 3% (not inaccurate, inflated figures of 10% or more).

Note: Even this 1-3% may be less because some cite a prison experience, college experimentation or one-time, drug-influenced encounter as part of "homosexual" background.

- *THE CAUSE OF HOMOSEXUALITY IS COMPLEX YET THERE ARE COMMON CONTRIBUTING FACTORS.*

    o   The person's self-will

    o   Dysfunctional home environment

    o   Spousal and child abuse

    o   Seduction by peers and authority figure (85% of lesbians were molested and 40% of gay men were seduced by older gay men when they were young boys").[68]

    o   Media influence

    o   Pornography

    o   Drugs

    o   Absence of a father

    o   Childhood experience/experimentation

    o   Confusion about identity/misunderstanding "artistic bent"

---

68   Louis P. Sheldon – President of Traditional Values Coalition

The National Association for Research and Therapy of Homosexuality (N.A.R.T.H.) states, "100% of their research participants said their father-figure was distant, uninvolved in their upbringing, frightening and unapproachable. 87% spoke of a mother who was close, controlling and overbearing."

Clinical psychologist, Joseph Nicolosi, Ph.D. who works in this field made this most interesting statement: "In 15 years, I have spoken with hundreds of homosexual men. I have never met one who said he had a loving, respectful relationship with his father."

Someone may offer an exception, but the overwhelming data points to problems in the home where a father doesn't bond properly with his son and a mother doesn't bond properly with her daughter.

- *SOME PEOPLE ARE DEFINITELY MORE SUSCEPTIBLE TO HOMOSEXUALITY THAN OTHERS (PROCLIVITY VS. PRACTICE).*

Some individuals are "wired" more towards these artistic areas: music, singing, dance, poetry, cooking, clothing-design, hairstyling, and painting as opposed to football, baseball, basketball, hunting, wrestling and other athletics. These differences are healthy and make for diversity in the human family. Yet, if a dad who enjoys contact sports ridicules a son who doesn't, or if a parent doesn't affirm a daughter's femininity, a child can feel misunderstood and rejected and most vulnerable to outside, negative influences.

One of my sons was more athletic, the other more artistic. I tried to affirm their bent with unconditional love, while helping both develop their masculinity. Today Justin is a single, Type A leader running aggressive, political campaigns. Jason is married, a worship leader and an outstanding, caring lead pastor of an Atlantan Church.

When I was growing up, I received good moral training and was involved in lots of athletics, even though my dad was more the artistic type (he loved singing, writing poetry, acting and films). When two male teenage relatives tried to seduce me into sexual experimentation as a youth, I had enough courage and common sense to resist. Likewise, when a homosexual picked me up hitchhiking and offered me money to come to his apartment for an enema (I was 13 and clueless as to what it was!), I am ever grateful that my upbringing and discernment prompted me to get out of that car! What could have happened to my life had things gone a different way?

Some closing points:

1. *There is a difference between DESIRE and DEED.* Many good people lay in their beds wrestling with "feelings" and fantasies regarding homosexuality. Just because someone is tempted in areas does not mean they are guilty of sexual misconduct. "You can't stop birds flying around your head, but you can stop them from building a nest in your hair!"

2. *Because someone doesn't "feel" there's anything wrong with homosexuality, doesn't make it right.*

    Objective standards not subjective feelings have to govern our lives or else people can justify all kinds of behavior – pedophilia, rape, child molestation, etc.

    Example: When Mel White, onetime ghostwriter for numerous influential religious leaders, decided to divorce his wife and enter into a homosexual relationship, he said he was "taking the first steps toward integrity." I wonder how his wife and family felt as Mel acted upon his feelings.

3. *While God loves all people, it is His plan to see us change to fulfill our destiny.* Jesus Christ "welcomed and accepted" everyone but called them to change unrighteous lifestyles – the adulteress, the multi-"lover" Samaritan, the corrupt tax collectors. He may not have used our book title's expression, but in essence He said it: "Here's the deal: 'Go and sin no more!'"[69]

4. *While Jesus Christ never specifically used the term "homosexuality" (He never used the words "pornography," "heroin," "incest," or "spousal abuse"* either), He taught, modeled and called people to live a chaste lifestyle aligned with the moral teachings of Scripture.

    He never contradicted or compromised issues of purity while affirming "for this cause shall a man leave his father and mother and be joined to his wife."[70] Also, the gospel of John 21:25 notes that we don't have all His words, so He could have addressed this subject more specifically.

---

69   Book of John, Chapter 8:11
70   Book of Matthew, Chapter 19:5

5. Homosexual behavior can be changed as evidenced by multitudes throughout America and in the Bible.

    I personally know a woman who left a lesbian lifestyle after 42 years and a male former homosexual who today is married with numerous children.

    Organizations helping homosexuals find freedom through compassionate counseling are filled with the testimonies of thousands real people who really have changed.

    - Alan Chambers, President of Exodus International, was himself, at one time a homosexual who was told by the gay community "there was no hope for change."

    - Actress Anne Heche left her homosexual partnership with Ellen DeGeneres to marry a man, as did singer Sinead O'Connor when she married Nick Sommerlad.

    - Three time MVP in the WNBA (Women's National Basketball Assoc.) and two time gold medalist Sheryl Swoopes actually did it in reverse! She was married and with an 8 year old when she decided to divorce her husband for her "lover," Alisa Scott.

    Going from "straight to gay" or "gay to straight" undermines the theory that sexual orientation is inherited and unchangeable. You might call this "inconvenient truth."

6. *There are different types of homosexuals: those "given over"[71] to the lifestyle (conscience seared) and those "looking over" the lifestyle (conscience dulled).*

    It's a sad reality that some militant homosexuals are so consumed with anger, bitterness and even despair, that they willingly infect others with HIV/AIDS as well as embrace a manifesto to wage war against those disagreeing with them.

A Self-styled 'Gay Revolutionary' Offers a Challenge to Straight America:

We shall sodomize your sons, emblems of your feeble masculinity, of your shallow dreams and vulgar lies. We shall seduce them in your schools, in your

---
71   Book of Romans, Chapter 1:24-27 (NIV)

dormitories, in you gymnasiums, in your locker rooms, in your sports arenas, in your seminaries, in your youth groups...wherever men are with men together. Your sons shall become our minions and do our bidding. They will be recast in our image. They will come to crave and adore us."

All churches who condemn us will be closed. Our holy gods are handsome young men.... We shall be victorious because we are fueled with the ferocious bitterness of the oppressed...."
— Michael Swift, Boston Gay
Community News, Feb. 15-21, 1987

Others who are "looking over" the lifestyle are not really "committed" to anything, they are experimenting, fantasizing or being titillated by a culture awash in pornography and so-called "sexual freedom." Some are jaded from numerous sexual experiences gone south and are vulnerable to "dabble in something different."

7. *To call oneself an authentic Christian and remain a practicing homosexual is a direct contradiction of Biblical teaching and contrary to the "abundant life" promised by Jesus Christ.*[72]

Just as Christian hatred is an oxymoron, so too is the term "Gay Christian." God offers forgiveness and freedom through His Son which is the good news (gospel) of the Christian message. According to the Christian faith, once a person responds to the gospel message in repentance and faith, he or she finds a new start[73] to then fulfill one's destiny in life. Even as Saul of Tarsus – a murderer – became Paul the apostle, great saint and missionary leader, Christianity asserts that God redeems repentant people who may be "homosexuals, adulterers, drunkards, idolaters, or whatever." It happened in the "San Francisco" of their day – Corinth, and has been repeated all over the world.[74]

This spiritual awakening and change happened to me. I was not involved in homosexuality but I once was a mixed-up, selfish, immoral rock star playing drums in a 60s band ironically called, "The Lost Souls." I formerly propagated the deluded philosophy behind our current mess. Now I want to be a part of helping clean it up.

---

72   Gospel of John, Chapter 10:10
73   Book of John, Chapter 3:1-20.
74   Book of Corinthians, Chapter 6:9-11.

As the famous hymn declares, "I once was lost – but now I'm found. Was blind but now I see."

Will you join me?

9

HOMOSEXUALITY AND THE FUTURE OF THE FAMILY II

"Don't Tear Down a Fence Until You Know Why It Was Put Up."
— African Proverb

WHAT ABOUT GAY MARRIAGE?

Buckle your seatbelt. Here we go! What a way to close out this book, huh?

HERE'S THE DEAL: Although millions are clueless, many are confused and multitudes come out with guns a-blazin' (on both sides), the reality is that not everyone in America has truly grasped the epic proportions of this issue. While it is a well-known fact that the overwhelming majority of adult Americans are opposed to gay marriage and over 72% of African-Americans support protecting marriage as a union between one man and one woman, the upcoming younger generation seems to be in a different place!

In a 2006 national "Youth Hot Button Issues" poll by Zogby International, 75 percent of high school seniors favored legal recognition of same-sex relationships – marriage or civil unions. Similarly, 75 percent oppose a constitutional amendment to ban same-sex marriage, and 63 percent support adoptions by gay couples. While we don't know exactly how the questions were worded, it appears – at least on the surface - that most teens don't see a problem with gay marriage.

Let's begin our discussion by making sure we're all in a peaceful posture of heart....

Now what is your recollection of the angriest, scariest confrontation you've ever seen? Is there one where someone flew into a rage – eyes bulging, nostrils flaring, veins popping, arms flailing and obscenities flying? On the sensitive photo-plate of your mind, can you still hear

"You *!#@I#3!" while bystanders bear-hugged the person in his steroid inflamed, out-of-control rage?

Do you remember years ago when baseball player George Brett charged out of the dugout after connecting on a Goose Gossage fastball for a home run, only to have the umpire disqualify it due to some illegal pine-tar on his bat? ESPN still loops the highlight two decades after the ultra-tense altercation took place. When Goose was inducted into the Hall of Fame in 2008 he exclaimed, "Whew. That still is the maddest I've ever seen a person get!"

Unfortunately some of the debate on gay marriage escalates to these white-hot levels. The scene resembles Brett restrained at home plate and the tone reminds one of those ugly, spit-flying, punch-throwing episodes of the Jerry Springer show.

Consider the following as we gain perspective on why this is such an emotional, hot-button issue.

- James Dobson, whose radio listeners number in the millions, called the battle over gay marriage, "our D-Day or Gettysburg or Stalingrad."

- "Gay marriage may be the most divisive issue to face America's faith community since slavery," declared attorney and author, Oliver Thomas, in *USA Today* (8/4/08).

- Donald Wildmon, leader of the influential American Family Association said in a recent newsletter (in reference to a ballot initiative on gay marriage): "The battle that now rages...will eventually come to your state. [This referendum] is one of the most important votes for the family in the history of our country!"

And finally, these remarks came from Court Justices – one state, one Supreme.

- "The California Supreme Court does not have the right to erase, then re-cast, the age-old definition of marriage, as virtually all societies have understood it, in order to satisfy its own contemporary notions of equality and justice."
                                        — California Supreme Court Associate
                                        Justice, Marvin R. Baxter.

- "The court today pretends that...we need not fear judicial imposition of homosexual marriage, as has recently occurred in Canada. ...DO NOT BELIEVE IT."
                                        — Justice Antonin Scalia

Whew. And we're gonna try to close out this chapter by examining the topic in a civil, charitable and clear-cut way?

Yep. So let's all pause, take a deep breath and revisit the meaning behind this famous maxim -

"Don't Tear Down a Fence Until You Know Why It Was Put Up."

                                        — **African Proverb**

HERE'S THE DEAL: Whether you cite "Mother Nature" or "Nature's God" (as our Founding Founders did), men and women are designed and function differently, complement and complete each other, and through the wonder of marital union are able to procreate with each other to perpetuate the cycle of life. When things are in order, there is beauty to this self-evident plan. When disregarded, things start getting somewhat strange.

The reality is as follows: The institution of marriage between a man and a woman has been the cornerstone of civilization for more than 6,000 years. It ensures the survival of the human race and over the millennia has been upheld as sacred throughout the world because it is the basic building block of society. Billions globally, of all the different religions, have this conviction: Marriage and family are of divine origin, not man's invention.

You may recall from your study of anthropology that the institution of marriage and family are considered "cultural absolutes." No culture functions without some sort of regulated and sanctioned union between a man and a woman. And not one culture in the entire history of humankind (including those few that have been relatively tolerant of homosexuality) has ever allowed "marriage" between members of the same sex as a norm for family life. Additionally, every major religion in the world forbids homosexual practice and marriage while eighty-six nations register homosexual sex as a crime (in seven countries it is punishable by death).

This issue is not trivial and recent developments represent some watershed events of which we need to be fully aware. Re-engineering our society by reshaping male/female roles, deconstructing marriage and redefining family, all constitute a seismic shift in Western civilization. It is not far-fetched to consider that this radical change could contribute to our downfall as a nation just as other nations have collapsed preceding us. This cultural landmine cannot be ignored. "Those who fail to learn the lessons of history are condemned to repeat them."

In 2008, the California Supreme Court by a vote of 4 to 3, overturned an electoral decision supported exclusively by over 4-1/2 million residents (52 of 58 counties were united) who explicitly affirmed marriage as being exclusively between one man and woman. Afterwards an article ran in Newsweek magazine applauding how four judges simply decided via one ruling to demolish the institution of marriage as it had been honored in custom and law for 6,000 years.

Anna Quindlen celebrated in her column that "the gay-marriage issue is over and love won." She went on to say "opponents were suggesting that civilization would crash and burn," but "for those wailing gay marriage as an invention of amoral modernism...." She went on to cite a second century Roman poet who mentioned a homosexual couples in Rome's heyday.

Stop! Anna do you realize that you just said?! You boast that there was proof of a homosexual "couple" in Rome but fail to tell, as Paul Harvey says, "the rest of the story" regarding what happened to that society as morals and marriage crumbled.

Renowned British Anthropologist, J. D. Unwin undertook a massive study years ago where he chronicled eighty-six different cultures throughout history. His research found the following: Every nation that rejected monogamy in marriage disintegrated morally in less than one generation.

CHILDREN'S LIVES ARE AT STAKE

Do you recall your worst nightmares as a child? I mean are there any images that you recollect that caused you to look quickly under the bed and pull the covers over your head to shield you from any approaching boogeyman figure?

For me it was twofold. First was that mean ole' green-faced wicked "Witch of the West" in Wizard of Oz. With her monkey entourage flying around her and her eerie pea-green face, I trembled when I'd replay her guttural cackle while she flew in hot pursuit of the red-slippered Dorothy. Boy, was it a sigh of relief when that house fell on her and her protruding legs curled up underneath signaling her demise. Remember?

The other terrifying image was that of the African natives living in the jungle behind the gargantuan, fort barrier protecting them from the gargantuan, King Kong. The 1930's classic in black and white was imbedded in my mind as I replayed over and over again what it must have been like to be stretched out and tied up to be offered as a sacrifice to the chest-thumping chimp. I can still see Fay Wray thrashing her body, screaming at decibel's highest level when the mighty Kong stomped onto the scene.

Human sacrifice is not a product of fiction. Historians record countless examples – one of which took place in a land called Canaan, thousands of years ago. The Hebrew/Christian scriptures cite the account of sacrificial human offerings made to the ancient pagan god Molech. The primary ones offered were little children who were "passed through" a fire to be sacrificed in this horrific way.

The immolation of children sickens any civilized people, especially when it is cloaked in religious garb as "worship" like it was by the morally degenerate Canaanites. Yet these reprobate people also engaged in other practices that were categorized as morally reprehensible by the rabbis and early church fathers such as Augustine and his contemporaries. Their basis for condemning these practices was the sacred writings of the Hebrew and Christian scriptures (not mere cultural whim).

As the rabbis noted in the midrashic work, Sifra, "A man would marry a man and a woman [would marry] a woman." For such offenses (child sacrifice and same-sex unions) these pagan people were justly "vomited out" of their land.[75]

What's worthy of note here is that in the Hebrew/Christian Bible, there is a specific juxtaposition between the prohibition of child sacrifice – "You shall not present any of your children to pass through to Molech...."[76] and the like prohibition of homosexual interrelationship in the very next verse, "You shall not lie with a man as one lies with a woman, it is an abomination."[77]

---

75   Book of Leviticus, Chapter 18:25
76   Book of Leviticus, Chapter 18:21
77   Book of Leviticus, Chapter 18:22

Why the link? Because in both of these instances two things were at stake, 1) The honor and holiness of God; and 2) The well-being and future upbringing of children. Neither can be minimized, but for the sake of our discussion let's look at the latter.

JUSTICE FOR CHILDREN

In all the debate concerning same-sex marriage, it is the children, the forgotten victims who often get overlooked or even deliberately ignored. Let's keep uppermost the welfare of these, our most precious ones. Let's not live in some alternate universe of theory, pipedreams and unreality but in the realm of "charity and clarity" as singer and activist, Bono, challenged us. Although some say many gays have no intention of bringing children into their relationship (remember they are sterile and unable to procreate due to natural order), it still is important to address these two points:

1. What message is being communicated to our children and future generations about what exactly is a marriage and family in society?

2. What is the best way to provide for children once they have come into the world?

First, what message are we communicating?

Children learn from what they see – not just from what they hear. "What you are speaks so loud I can't hear what you say."

Let's get real: With all the troubles facing families in America today, this is not the time for trying some new, radical social experimentation. There are entire generations at stake. Reflect for a moment on the 60's "welfare state" idea that in the end proved to be an absolute disaster. This experiment caused wholesale disintegration among low-income families and sent the rate of black illegitimacy and fatherlessness skyrocketing. An underclass emerged plagued by violence, crime, joblessness, educational failure and multigenerational dependency. Initially, "progressives" said, "Hey, let's try this approach. What can we lose?"

The same thing happened when we foolishly thought in the late 60's that "no fault divorce" would improve marriage and family life.

Today the conclusive finding from research on three decades of this experiment bear out that it also has been a massive failure for couples, children and America at large. According to the "Statistical Abstract of the United States," the number of divorces in the U.S. has increased by 279% and the number of children living with a divorced parent has increased 352% since this "liberating" initiative took effect in 1970. Demographer, Dr. Paul Glick warns that one-third of all children will now live in a step-family arrangement before their 18th birthday!

Or, how about some of the radical feminist ideas touted in the 60's "counter-revolution" as women were encouraged to burn their bras (I'm not kidding!) and declare liberation from the "prison of domestic captivity!"[78] Ms. Magazine Editor, Gloria Steinham, probably the most visible and vocal of the "fem-theorists" once declared, "A woman needs a husband like a fish needs a bicycle!" (Pssstt! As her fame faded and her ideas evaporated, she quietly got married in her sixties. Someone quipped, "Evidently that fish decided she needed a bicycle!")

Author and Prison Fellowship Founder, Chuck Colson, wrote this piece on the "Legacy of Radical Feminism:"

FEMINISM'S CONSEQUENCES

"Alice Walker, best known as the author of the novel 'The Color Purple,' is one of the most renowned feminist authors and activists of her generation. She is also a mother*, and that fact brought her public and private lives into direct conflict.*

"That is because Alice Walker's brand of feminism was the kind that taught that 'motherhood was about the worst thing that could happen to a woman.' So says her daughter, Rebecca, who suffered the consequences of that thinking. In a recent London 'Daily Mail' article, Rebecca Walker reflected on the neglect she experienced with her divorced father across the country and her mother too busy for her, frequently leaving her alone for long periods as a teenager. With her mother's knowledge – and even support – Rebecca became sexually active at 13 and had an abortion at 14. She was well aware that her mother thought of her as a burden.

"The younger Walker – who lives in England – writes now, 'My mother's feminist principles coloured every aspect of my life. As a little girl, I wasn't even allowed to play with dolls or

stuffed toys in case they brought out a maternal instinct. It was drummed into me that being a mother, raising children and running a home were a form of slavery. Having a career, travelling the world and being independent were what really mattered according to her.'

"After years of private and public feuding, their estrangement is so deep that Alice has never yet even seen Rebecca's own son, her grandson. In an early interview, Rebecca suggested that this was the natural result of putting 'ideology' before relationships.

"As an African-American woman born in 1944, Alice Walker saw her share of injustices. Her instinct to try to put things right was not the problem there. The problem was that she was part of a generation of feminists who believed that the way to correct injustice was to put yourself first and everyone else, including your family, last. Women taught their daughters this by both precept and by example. And as a result, Rebecca says now, 'Feminism has betrayed an entire generation of women into childlessness. It is devastating.'

"Rebecca has met many women who avoided having children because they thought that it was their duty to do so, and now are despondent that it is no longer possible for them to do so."[79]

HERE'S THE DEAL: Throughout thousands of years of history (allowing for a few strange exceptions), the normal, natural, ideal arrangement and definition of a family is a group of heterosexual individuals, "male and female" related to each other by marriage, with children by birth or adoption. For over six-thousand years this standard has remained since the initial mandate was given to, "Be fruitful and multiply."[80]

For those who object saying, "This is too narrow," let's remind ourselves that truth is narrow: 1 and 1 is always 2! Two elements of hydrogen and 1 of oxygen are always water! Pilots always land planes on "narrow" runways versus any ole' place under the sun!

For those who say "marriage doesn't have to *only* mean the joining of two people of the opposite sex," keep in mind that if this is removed, "marriage" as we've known it for millennia becomes meaningless (or defined anyway any one wants to). Removing an entire sex out of

---

79   Breakpoint Commentary, 6/27/08.
80   Book of Genesis, Chapter 1:27-28.

marriage and calling it "marriage" is like removing chocolate from a chocolate cake recipe. It's no longer the same thing!

MARRY A PONY?

For those wishing to tamper with the truth by elasticizing the definition to "whatever one feels," consider the implications. If the term marriage and family designates any arrangement, where do we draw the line? If a man and three ladies are fine, we'll have to resurrect the debate from the 1800's outlawing polygamy. If a woman feels inclined to "marry" her adult son, is this okay? How about marriage to your favorite llama or darling horse. (Preposterous? Check out the 1995 Missouri case where 'Mark' "fell in love" with Pixel, his beloved pony, and attempted to "marry" her in a private ceremony!)

One more thought. Instead of simply a single "same sex" arrangement, what would we answer to three gay men wanting to all be married (to each other) along with a lesbian lover and one or two bisexuals joining the "circle of love?"

Do you see how dangerous this line of thinking really is? Marriage is the building block of a culture – it is sacred – not simply another morally neutral entity like stamp collecting or bird watching.

Barbara Bush, wife of George Sr. and former First Lady of the United States, spoke the following wisdom in a commencement speech at Wellesby College in 1990, "Your success as a family…our success as a society depends not on what happens in the White House, but on what happens inside your house." How true. As the family goes, so goes the nation.

Marrying and staying married, then having children and being responsible for them, these are the values that built and sustained our country and countries throughout the millennia. While divorce, out-of-wedlock births, barrenness and desertion admittedly tarnish the picture, by seeking the ideal yet facing the real we stay on course. Our children witness the institution of marriage between a man and woman as the cornerstone of civilization for over 6,000 years and are secure that this arrangement remains constant for their provision and protection. We all benefit by not succumbing to the proverbial Pandora's Box that would jettison the sacred covenant of marriage to placate the sexual proclivities of a miniscule minority in our country.

One of the most beloved popes in history was Pope John Paul (a Polish man – 3 cheers!). His heart for justice came through with these poignant words in his inspiring Vatican document on this theme:

"Homosexual unions are totally lacking in the biological and anthropological elements of marriage and family which would be the basis, on the level of reason, for granting them legal recognition. Such unions are not able to contribute in a proper way to the procreation and survival of the human race."

The secondly point essential to address is this - "What is the best way to provide for children?"

Presently the state of marriage and the family have become unstable and even fragile since the 60's season of "throwing off restraints." While there are options today for gay and lesbian "partnerships," to go beyond this to formally sanction same-sex marriage is very dangerous.

Many have recognized the state of the family in our society and are working diligently to strengthen the family and remedy the problem ("Thanks Bill Cosby for being one of the pioneers!"). Better pre-marital counseling, on-going enrichment classes and even "renewal of covenant marriage" couple's events all contribute to a healing restorative mix.

If we acquiesce to homosexual marriage and do with marriage and family what we did with welfare and "no fault divorce," families will be less stable, divorce will be higher, children will be less safe and the moral plus financial fallout will be incalculable.

We would do better to "shore up" what has been lacking while reminding ourselves of the benefits to children and society of upholding the historic view of marriage and family.

HERE'S THE DEAL: In spite of all the flaws – particularly those resulting from 60's experimentation – the age-old institution of marriage and the natural family are best for providing happiness to couples and offspring and for nurturing children. A loving father and mother (not merely "loving partners") properly complement each other in the child-raising experience instead of intentionally depriving children of the dad and mom they need. Unfortunately, where there is a divorce, at least there usually remains the father and mother component although admittedly in a less than ideal way.

Studies by even pro-homosexual researchers reveal that children in gay households are more likely to experiment sexually, break gender norms and identify as homosexual or bisexual than children reared in traditional homes.

- The *American Journal of Orthopsychiatry* (4/95) published that 24% of children raised by lesbian mothers had "been involved in a same-gender sexual relationship."

- In a 1994 article in *American Sociological Review*, Dr. Judith Stacey, a sociologist at the University of Southern California, said: "The young adults reared by lesbian mothers were also significantly more likely to report having thought they might experience homoerotic attraction or relationships." The differences were "striking," she added, "because 64% of the young adults raised by same-sex parents said they had considered having a same-sex relationship."

- A Tasker-Golombok study, "Adults Raised as Children in Lesbian Families," revealed that the percentage of the young women raised by lesbians who later went on to self-identify as lesbians was nearly eight-times the rate of the general population (11% versus 1.4%).

Let's get real – the most "loving" lesbian in the world cannot teach a boy how to be a man any more than the most "loving" gay man cannot teach a girl how to be a woman (although both will teach them a lot about "other things" by their daily influence along with exposing them to homosexual behavior on a regular basis).

Imagine two gay dads leading their daughter through her first "period"… explaining female issues she's encountering…what to look for in a "training bra" or how about a future husband…explaining to her why her "dads" act, talk and relate as they do.

Imagine two lesbians trying to instruct their son about throwing a football… answering embarrassing male sexual inquiries…explaining why they sleep together…handling potential razzing he gets from his friends (children can be cruel and could care less about being politically correct)…helping him buy a jock strap, handle a bully or learn how to defend himself…learn what to look for in a wife and then how to care for her.

Kay Hymowitz of the "Manhattan Institute Think Tank" told The *Economist* publication, "Middle class kids growing up with two biological parents are 'socialized for success.' They do better in school, get better jobs and go on to create intact families of their own."

Question: **"What about the situation where the choice is between having homosexual parents or no parents at all?"**

The truth is there are hundreds of thousands of husband-and-wife couples waiting seven to ten years, desperately wanting to adopt children. It's a straw man to use this argument to support gay marriage and gay adoptions.

Question: **"Aren't two gay parents better than one single parent?"**

In the overwhelming majority of single parent households, children still benefit from the father and mother dynamic – imperfect as it may be. Children interact with both sexes, they have their presence and input as they develop and observe male and female role models. Also, many single parents do remarry!

Children develop healthiest and learn crucial things that prepare them for life when they can observe interactions and differences in married, father-mother, households. Human experience and the vast body of social science research demonstrate what should be a "no-brainer."

In his book, "Homosexual Parenting: Placing Children at Risk," Dr. Timothy Dailey concluded: *"The complementary aspects of parenting that mothers and fathers contribute to the rearing of children are rooted in the innate differences of the two sexes, and can no more be arbitrarily substituted than can the very nature of male and female. [Indeed, despite] accusations of sexism and homophobias..., [despite] attempts to deny the importance of both mothers and fathers in the rearing of children, the oldest family structure of all turns out to be the best."*

HERE'S THE DEAL: Justice demands that we not sit silently on the sidelines but speak up lest a small percentage of homosexuals (1-3% of the population) and their sympathizers destroy the institution of time-honored marriage and family. The reason (let's get real): to satisfy sexual appetites and pursue selfish individualism, all at the expense of innocent children for whose future we are responsible.

HERE'S THE DEAL: Children are the victims when adults steamroll over them for abortion-on-demand, no-fault divorce legislation and now attempts to legitimize gay marriage. We all can see the devastating results in Norway, Sweden and Denmark, where redefining traditional marriage has brought the disintegration of marriage along with astronomical leaps in the out-of-wedlock birth rate. Our children must not watch America put its official stamp of approval on homosexual marriage, learning this is all "normal," "natural" – simply an "alternative" lifestyle choice. Justice demands we take care of millions of precious kids, not deny them a proper family experience.

Think of this from another angle. The skyrocketing jail and prison population today is continuing to escalate. Let's ask ourselves, "Where did it come from?

The fact is, all the social experimentation stemming from the mid-60's "revolution" brought about a tragic breakdown of the family. Where children weren't properly trained, learned character, taught how to make moral choices and how to respect laws and authority, many drifted into drugs and crime.

Who helped facilitate this? It was us baby-boomers who proudly called ourselves "The 'Me' Generation," yet now see the folly of our youthful ways.

I read recently of a study of an inner-city district where 90% of the youth from broken families got into trouble. Intact families saw only 6% of their youth get into trouble. Here's the deal: Crime comes from people making wrong moral choices and oftentimes they come from dysfunctional families. It is in healthy families where children have the optimum chance to learn to make right choices. To say otherwise is simply downright dishonest!

People concerned with justice will not ignore our current societal problems nor will we act foolishly to compound them by further weakening the state of marriage and family by legalizing gay marriage.

Supreme Court Justice Antonin Scalia has said,

"Many Americans do not want persons who openly engage in homosexual conduct as partners in their business, as scoutmasters for their children, as teachers in their children's schools or as boarders in their home.... They view this as protecting themselves and their families from a life style that they believe to be immoral and destructive."

IN THEIR OWN WORDS

For those who are still naïve to the agenda of homosexual activists, pause and listen to how some in their midst state their case.

"A middle ground might be to fight for same-sex marriage and its benefits and then, once granted, redefine the institution of marriage completely, to demand the right to marry not as a way of adhering to society's moral codes but rather to debunk a myth and radically alter an archaic institution."[81]

And there's this from pro-homosexual and pro-pedophile author Judith Levine (she favors lowering the age of consent to 12 for sex between children and adults):

"Because American marriage is inextricable from Christianity, it admits participants as Noah let animals onto the ark. But it doesn't have to be that way. In 1972, the National Coalition of Gay Organizations demanded the 'repeal of all legislative provisions that restrict the sex or number of persons entering into a marriage unit; and the extension of legal benefits to all persons who cohabit regardless of sex or numbers.' Would polygamy invite abuse of child brides, as feminists in Muslim countries and prosecutors in Mormon Utah charge? No. Group marriage could comprise any combination of genders."

STOP AND THINK

What are the implications of gay marriage, gay adoptions and other gay, lesbian, bi-sexual and trans-gender initiatives for *you*? I mean, let's bring this home – out of the theoretical into the practical. Consider a few very real scenarios for **you, your** children and **your** future.

- Do you want educators in your child's school discussing and showing textbook photos and DVDs of same-sex couples as "normal" in required "sensitivity training" classes?

- Do you want same-sex neighbors and their children inviting your children to come over and play or join the sleepover at their house?

- How would you handle your daughter bringing home her "date"

---

81   Michelangelo Signorile, "Bridal Wave," OUT Magazine, Dec./Jan. 1994, p. 161.

– a young fella' who was raised in a home with two lesbian "parents?"

- If you own a business, could you afford the health care benefits for 4 or 5 people declaring themselves "married" in a same-sex, group marriage?

- What would you do if your young daughter went to the public restroom and came out rattled because there was a man inside who upon inquiry, stated he was "transgender" – a person of one sex who perceive themselves to be of the other sex? Or what if you as a woman were taking a shower after your aerobics class only to find a man showering next to you? This now can happen. (Our former hometown of Montgomery County, MD passed a law in 2007 – as did the entire state of Colorado – opening all public accommodations to "transgendered people," so as not to be "discriminatory" and allowing for situations such as the above. Governor Ritter of Colorado signed it into law while a referendum has been called in Montgomery CO due to concerned citizens.)

- How would you feel if your beloved pastor or rabbi made comments in a sensitive way yet opposed to homosexuality and was placed in jail for "hate-speech" pronouncements viewed as "intolerant and discriminatory?"

This has already happened in other counties and there are those who want it coming your way.

These are just some of the very real and catastrophic effects of the whole gay marriage push. And bear in mind, acceptance of gay marriage "rights" provides momentum for changing other liberties. Columnist Jennifer Morse stated in the National Catholic Register,

"Legalizing same-sex 'marriage' is not a stand-alone policy.... Once governments assert that same-sex unions are the equivalent of marriage, those governments must defend and enforce a whole host of other social changes."

- This is why Catholic Charities of Massachusetts was ordered to accept homosexual couples as adoption candidates. (By the way, they closed down their adoption program rather than comply.)

- This is why Associate Vice President of the University of Toledo, Crystal Dixon, was fired after she penned an op-ed in the Toledo-Free Press in support of traditional marriage.

- This is why a Methodist retreat center in New Jersey had its tax-exempt status revoked after refusing to allow lesbian couples its usage for civil union ceremony.

- This is why a 39 year old Michigan gay man has launched federal lawsuits against the two Christian publishing grants, Zondervan (for $60 million) and Thomas Nelson (for $10 million) stating "discrimination" that led him to "suffer emotional pain, mental instability and estrangement from family" in their citing of homosexuality as sin.

- This is why parents are withdrawing scores of children from public schools in California after Senate Bill 777 mandated that teachers teach different sexual orientations as all valid and equal. Since California and Texas are number 1 and number 2 in national sales of textbooks to schools, guess what will soon be a part of your children's curriculum in the coming years (unless people awaken and stand firm)?

These are not isolated horror stories. They're real. And if you think people are merely "playing games" when it comes to these issues, contact talk-show host and author, Dr. Laura Schlessenger, whose entire TV show was cancelled because she had the audacity to suggest that homosexuality is a biological abnormality.

Are you catching the drift? Gay marriage is not really about "tolerance," "equality" and "progress," it's about disregarding privacy and decency to pressure everyone to embrace the homosexual agenda or else.

A PERSONAL TESTIMONY

Take a moment and read a first person account from a young Canadian woman raised in a same-sex household.

EYEWITNESS TO DEBAUCHERY
Canadian Woman Reveals what it was Like Growing Up in
A Same-Sex Household, and Why Gay Adoption is a Bad Idea

My name is Dawn Stefanowicz. I grew up in a homosexual household during the 1960s and 1970s in Toronto exposed to many different people, the Gay-Lesbian-Bisexual-Transgendered (GLBT) subcultures, and explicit sexual practices.

My biggest concern is that children are not being discussed in this same-sex marriage debate. Yet, won't the next step for some gay activists be to ask for legal adoption of children if same-sex marriage is legalized? I have considered some of the potential physical and psychological health risks for children raised in this situation. I was at high risk of exposure to contagious STDs due to sexual molestation, my father's high-risk sexual behaviors, and multiple partners. Even when my father was in what looked like monogamous relationships, he continued cruising for anonymous sex.

My father's (ex)partners, whom I had deep caring feelings for and associated with, had drastically shortened lives due to suicide, contracting HIV or AIDS. Sadly, my father died of AIDS in 1991.

Are my childhood experiences unique? According to a growing number of personal testimonies, experts, and organizations, there is mounting evidence of strong commonalities to my personal experiences. Not only do children do best with both a mother and a father in a lifelong marriage bond, children need responsible monogamous parents who have no extramarital sexual partners.

From a young age, I was exposed to explicit sexual speech, self-indulgent lifestyles, varied GLBT subcultures and gay vacation spots. Sex looked gratuitous to me as a child. I was exposed to all-inclusive manifestations of sexuality including bathhouse sex, cross-dressing, sodomy, pornography, gay nudity, lesbianism, bisexuality, minor recruitment, voyeurism and exhibitionism. Sado-masochism was alluded to and aspects demonstrated. Alcohol and drugs were often contributing factors to lower inhibitions in my father's relationships.

Over two decades of direct exposure to these stressful experiences caused me insecurity, depression, suicidal thoughts, dread, anxiousness, low self-esteem, sleeplessness and sexuality confusion. My conscience and innocence were seriously damaged. I witnessed that every other family member suffered severely as well.

I believe same-sex marriage will dispose of unique values

esteemed within marriage as recognized throughout history. Marriage needs to remain a societal foundation that constitutes, represents and defends the inherently procreative relationship between the husband and the wife for the welfare of their biological children.

Why does such a small, unrepresentative clique within the GLBT subcultures want same-sex marriage? Mr. John McKellay, executive director of H.O.P.E., (Homosexuals Opposed to Pride Extremism) has stated:

> *"It is selfish and rude for the gay community to push same-sex marriage legislation and redefine society's traditions and conventions for our own self-indulgence.... Federal and provincial laws are being changed and the traditional values are being compromised just to appease a tiny, self-anointed clique."*

THE FINAL DEAL

HERE'S THE *FINAL* DEAL: Because certain behaviors undermine the foundations of the family, the cornerstone of society, the State must exercise its restrictive powers for the common good. This is not discrimination – it is protection. While all Americans have a privilege of the "pursuit of happiness," this does not mean pursuit without limitations. Adultery, prostitution, polygamy, child molestation and endangerment, failure to pay child support are all subject to state control. Same-sex marriage belongs in this category.

Abraham Lincoln said in his 1863 Gettysburg Address that America is a system of government designed "of the people, by the people, and for the people." At this defining moment in history, we must not tolerate any small, elite group of arrogant judges slamming down a gavel to rule against the masses and thousands of years of human history-honoring marriage exclusively as that between a man and woman. They must not be allowed to launch a radical social experiment redefining marriage as virtually all societies have understood it, open a door to polygamy, group marriage and whatever, as well as legitimize homosexual behavior in the eyes of children for generations to come. We must not let this dye be cast.

Let's display the same type of courage a national audience saw when Park Gillespie competed on the Showtime reality series, "American

Candidate." He won the $200,000 first prize and then delivered his unedited "acceptance" speech to the nation. Here's what he bravely communicated on nationwide T.V.

"Jefferson warned of an oligarchy, the rule of a few; he taught us that without the consent of the governed, those who govern have no moral or legal authority. And that's just what we're on the verge of creating in this country. Unelected, unaccountable judges are making laws the people would never pass. For example, wherever voters have had the chance to speak on same-sex marriage – by supermajorities in Alaska and Nevada, Hawaii and Louisiana, Missouri and California – they have affirmed the institution as the union of one man and one woman. That's the way it's supposed to be in a government of the people, by the people, for the people.

"Legalizing same-sex marriage – which Massachusetts did this year and which every state in the union could be forced to do if the judicial tyrants have their way – could strike a crippling blow to families. Study after study has found that boys and girls not raised by both their biological parents are much more likely to suffer abuse, perform poorly in school, abuse drugs and alcohol and wind up in trouble with the law.

"Did our Founders fight and die to wrest their liberty from a tyrannical king, only to hand it to a group of black-robed judges? Should the desires of adults ever trump what's best for kids? The needs of our most vulnerable must come first."

THE CHALLENGE

All of us must work peacefully and diligently for the sake of justice.

If necessary (and it probably is) we should with honorable elected officials work to enact a Constitutional amendment to protect the sanctity of marriage in America and the moral foundations upon which our country was founded. When the Emancipation Proclamation was written, it was still necessary to avert loopholes in legislation and insure that slavery would be outlawed in every state, so a constitutional amendment was enacted. The time may have arrived to do this once again. Whatever it takes, we will act respectfully but unitedly to strengthen not further destabilize the institution of marriage in the United States of America.

Our first President, George Washington, communicated in his farewell address what was central to making this nation great. We stand on his shoulders with our children securely upon ours, in reaffirming his position: "Of all the dispositions and habits which lead to political prosperity, religion and morality are indispensable supports."

As responsible citizens of this nation, we add our "Amen" and say our farewell.

That's the deal!

Sincerely,
Larry
& Melanie
Tomczak

10 Reasons Why Same-sex Marriage Is Wrong

— **Larry Tomczak**

1. It violates the clear and unambiguous moral teaching of the Hebrew Christian Scriptures which serve as the basis for our Judeo-Christian laws and foundations as a nation.

2. It is contradictory to the self-evident truth of "Mother Nature" or "Nature's God" (as our Founding Fathers expressed it) wherein men and women are designed and function differently, complement and complete each other, and through the wonder of marital union are able to procreate with each other to perpetuate the cycle of life.

3. It is contrary to the explicit teaching of every major world religion which upholds the integrity of marriage and family.

4. It undermines the institution of marriage between a man and a woman that has been the cornerstone of civilization in custom and law for more than 6,000 years of human history.

5. Not one civilized culture in the entire history of mankind (including those few that have been relatively tolerant of homosexuality) has ever allowed "marriage" between members of the same sex as a norm for family life.

6. It is an injustice and unequivocally harmful, selfish arrangement wherein our most precious entrustment, our children, are denied the love and nurture of a father and a mother who complement each other in healthy family life.

7. It redefines and devalues the sacred institution of marriage exclusively between a man and a woman in addition to opening the door for other arrangements such as polygamy, group marriage and even bestiality.

8. It is a radical social experiment like the disastrous "welfare state" and "no fault divorce" ideas, which must not be embraced lest we further destabilize the already fragile family – the basic building block of our society.

9. It legitimizes, normalizes and places an official stamp of approval on a lifestyle replete with dangerous, at-risk sexual behavior such as HIV/AIDS and over thirty STDs that are endangering lives, jeopardizing health care and impacting our economy.

10. It is opposed by the overwhelming majority of our nation who are decent, hard-working citizens and rightfully angry at arrogant, unelected, unaccountable judges imposing their radical redefinition of marriage and family upon us.

"As the family goes – so goes the nation."

Other books you will enjoy
by Larry Tomczak

- Clap Your Hands

- Why Wait Til Marriage?

- Divine Appointments

- Reckless Abandon

- So What Do You Believe?

- Little Handbook on Loving Correction

- Happily Ever After

www.HeresTheDeal.cc